# The Future of the
# Medical Plastics Market

# The Future of the Medical Plastics Market
## Opportunities for Growth

Vincent Sabourin, Ph.D.

Full-time Professor of Strategy and Innovation
Management ESG UQAM and Chairman
Consortium Innovation

Routledge
Taylor & Francis Group

A PRODUCTIVITY PRESS BOOK

First published 2022
by Routledge
605 Third Avenue, New York, NY 10158

and by Routledge
2 Park Square, Milton Park, Abingdon, Oxon, OX14 4RN

*Routledge is an imprint of the Taylor & Francis Group, an informa business*

© 2022 Vincent Sabourin

*Library of Congress Cataloging-in-Publication Data*
A catalog record for this book has been requested

ISBN: 978-1-032-08092-5 (hbk)
ISBN: 978-1-032-08091-8 (pbk)
ISBN: 978-1-003-21289-8 (ebk)

DOI: 10.4324/9781003212898

Typeset in Garamond
by Apex CoVantage, LLC

# Contents

xiv ■ *Contents*

# About the Author

Vincent Sabourin is a full-time professor of business strategy and innovation management at the School of Management (ESG) of the University of Quebec in Montreal (UQAM). He teaches at various levels of executive MBA, including the MBA for science and engineering.

He has served as the project director in "Promising Plastics and Advanced Materials Opportunities" for a Canadian Federation of Plastic Producers. He has been a keynote speaker for several conferences on advanced plastics, smart technologies, and the Internet of Things.

Dr. Sabourin is the chairman of the Consortium Innovation, a non-profit organization and a collaborative network in innovation and management. As a strategy expert, he advises businesses and the government. He was one of 25 Canadian experts in the business strategy selected for a doctoral dissertation at HEC Montréal. He has published several books, book chapters, academic articles, and proceedings in management innovation and new technologies.

Professor Sabourin is also honored with a diploma in industrial psychology from the University of McGill, a master's degree in administration from HEC Montréal, and a PhD in planning and strategic management at McGill University, under the supervision of Henry Mintzberg.

# About Consortium Innovation

Consortium Innovation is a Canadian non-profit organization producing and diffusing applied research in the area of innovation management. The NGO collaborates with industries and research centers. The Consortium also works with several organizations such as trade associations and research centers, particularly CEFRIO, Canadian plastic trade associations, Plastipolis, and the French Plastic trade association.

Consortium Innovation produces and diffuses market studies, e-books, reports, and handbooks for industries and research centers to understand better the transformation provided by digital technologies. The organization is active in science and technology, particularly in artificial intelligence, digital innovations, the Internet of things, and advanced materials. Consortium Innovation feels proud to collaborate with aeronautics, hydroelectricity and energy, fashion and clothing, building and construction, plastic, and telecom.

# Introduction

Plastics have occupied an important place in the modern medical industry. It has substituted traditional devices and products made of metal, other materials, and ceramics. In recent years, increased reliance on transparent plastic pharmaceutical and medical products has produced remarkable breakthroughs that improve medical attention delivery and allow it to be more comfortable, helping the masses live better and longer lives.

The purpose of this market report is to provide a strategic perspective on the market to identify opportunities for growth and promising niches in the medical plastics market. It also analyzes emerging trends in medical plastics to facilitate new product development.

# Study Objectives

The medical plastics market is a new field with a broad scope and unending opportunities for manufacturers and suppliers and medical practitioners from healthcare. With a combination of the right material and technology, it has a lot to offer to the patients with affordable pricing. By keeping the worth of the medical plastics market in mind, we have set some objectives. They are as follows:

- To present a background on the medical plastics market by its usage, products, processes, and innovation
- To review existing studies on the medical plastics market for topics like market size, market growth, segment growth, and geographic markets
- To identify growth defining factors in the medical plastics market
- To analyze critical factors of success to compete in the medical plastics market
- To identify promising niches and analyze the business opportunities
- To assess in detail the attractiveness of the market for new products, new distribution channels, and new geographic markets, and the development of new strategic competencies
- To evaluate the structure of the competition and find opportunities for investors and key players

- To examine the strategic context for the medical plastics market to recognize opportunities and challenges
- To appraise critical research for new applications and product development
- To track emerging topics for new R&Ds
- To profile and document the strategy of market leaders

# Research Methodology

The study is based on analyzing the five hundred most essential information sources from 2015 to 2020 for the medical plastics market. The following information sources were used to make this market report:

- Trade journals such as *Plastic News*, *Plastics Today*, Plastic Research, and new materials;
- Meta-analysis and review of existing studies such as world markets research, Market and Markets, Sheet Analytics and Insights, Business Wire, Bccresearch.com, and IBISWorld;
- Corporate documents of 25 companies who are the leaders in the medical plastics market and public reports from research institutes and centers in medical plastics;
- Survey of the ten hottest topics of research publications with the SciVal indicator and an analysis of 150 significant research publications in the last five years for the plastic medical market in scientific papers in English, German and French;
- Documents from OECD, the European Commission, and the American, German, French, Australian, and Canadian governments regarding policies for the medical plastics market;

■ Analysis of the market and competition with the following three tools developed by the Consortium Innovation:

■ The strategic context index (CC Index) which provides a review of the market's strategic context's opportunities and threats;

■ The index of the market potential (IMP Index) which assesses investors' market potential or existing players;

■ The Industry Attractiveness Index (IA Index) which measures and assesses the industry's attractiveness and competition structure.

## Chapter 1

# Overview of the Plastics Market

Plastic could be described as any substance that is an element of an enormous range of synthetic or semi-synthetic solid materials used in creating manufacturing products.

Plastics are polymers that include a top molecular mass and sometimes include other substances to enhance the look and maybe functionality and lower manufacturing costs. The term *plastic* has its roots in the Greek term *plastikos*, which means capable of being molded or shaped.

Plastic material is appreciated for being extremely malleable and capable of being machined, cast, extruded, or even pressed into an assortment of styles.

Over the years, the medical plastics market has made progress by introducing advanced plastics in the pharmaceutical market. Polymers are utilized in artificial organs, surgery, or medicine in three ways:

- to create total synthetic substitutes for human organs
- to restore, experience, or maybe augment characteristics of regular organs
- to make a biochemical feature

DOI: 10.4324/9781003212898-1

1

Plastic is commonly used in the production of several types of medical equipment. Artificial hearts, heart–lung devices, and artificial kidneys are good examples of synthetic organs developed to replace natural organs.

Plastics have a range of attributes required for these applications, including ease of fabrication, substance inertness, and non-toxic qualities, along with a broad range of actual physical characteristics in hardness, freedom, and permeability.

Plastics in medicine have increased the quality of life for older adults and those injured in accidents. Today's artificial hips and knees depend on plastics to provide individuals with pain-free movement as well as trouble-free joints. The gloves that surgeons wear are made from very soft and pliable plastics, keeping the hospital environment sterile. Plastics tackle healthcare needs small and large, from dishes in the laboratory to the housing of extensive analysis healthcare machinery.

These innovations provide extra cost savings through medical care and equipment usage. In addition, innovations that may be supplied as lightweight, robust, and straightforward health products are now developed for individuals in a home environment.

## Health-Related Plastics and Medical Costs

The integration of plastic into modern medicine has progressively risen within the past ten years. Health-related plastics have considerably reduced medical costs. Advanced polymers are adopted to manufacture new as well as enhanced artificial limbs. For example, in disposable products, plastic has become essential in making disposable delivery products, which are crucial in limiting disease threat to individuals. This progress is achieved with medical devices.

In developing a medical unit wherein assembly is needed, manufacturers consider the component layout and the assembly process, the standard style, and procedure management. Design, part size, material, geometry, and end-user specifications have become essential to improve the quality of the product at large.

# Growth Overview

Several factors explain the growth of plastics in the medical market.

## *Plastics as Substitutes*

Plastic has substituted for numerous products in the design of medical devices, and there has been an exponential improvement in the mechanical and physical properties of a polymer. It can compete with metal, and the convergence toward this material is already underway.

Numbers of medical plastics are incomparable and superior to traditional materials because they are resistant, lightweight, cheaper, more flexible, and more comfortable. Medical polymers have become a significant element of medical devices leading to the emergence of a new generation of medical technology.

## *Toward Safer and Simpler Medical Methods*

Plastics' utilization brings a revolution in medicine, rendering individuals safer and methods more straightforward. An excellent example of this is the use of the magnetic resonance image (MRI). An MRI is basically a massive magnet that can draw in some metal items within its range. Metal objects situated near the MRI machine might be dangerous and should be lightweight in case they are attracted by the magnetized device. Today, an MRI's gear is produced from transparent plastic to guard against this risk. Even tools utilized to set up the MRI are fabricated from plastic.

### The Value-Added of Plastic in Medical Devices

In developing a medical unit wherein assembly is needed, manufacturers should consider the component layout and the assembly process, the standard style, and procedure management.

# Scope of Plastic Products in the Medical Market

Plastics generally include polyethylene, polypropylene, poly-olefins, polyethylene terephthalate, polyethylene terephthalate G, and vinyl chloride. The scope of plastic products in the medical market includes comprehensive product lines and plastic packaging systems such as:

- Bags
- Cartridges
- Nebulizers
- Syringes
- Vials
- Bottles
- Capsules and tablets

## Thermoplastic Polymer Elastomers for Medical and Pharmaceutical Applications

Thermoplastic polymer elastomers (TPE) are mainly used for medical and pharmaceutical applications such as tour-niquets, medical films, drip chambers, and connectors. TPE are compounds of high purity that are not very susceptible to filtration and extraction. These qualities are required to ensure patient safety. Moreover, flexibility, lifetime, neutrality, and ease of recycling make it a simple alternative to PVC and thermo-hardened rubber for medical tubes. Also, TPE is more gas impermeable and more flexible than silicon at a lower cost.

Moreover, its transparency and high capacity to resist the different sterilization methods (gamma, ethylene oxide, and steam) are appreciated by the specialists.

# Benefits of Medical Plastics

Medical plastics provide a full range of benefits to stakeholders and healthcare service providers.

## *Improving Medical Equipment*

Due to its eco-friendly nature, healthcare polymers help improve medical kit material and diagnostic systems. More specifically, the increasing demand for medical devices due to the rising number of heart diseases, common illnesses, and infections are the main factors behind the tremendous market growth of medical polymers worldwide.

## *Increasing Health Awareness*

Increasing health awareness among developed countries currently also supports the industry.

## *Increasing Global Geriatric Population*

Moreover, globally, the increasing market size of the aged population is a weighty factor behind the growing need for medical products. We review this critical trend in more detail throughout the book.

## Market Size and Growth

We could rely on several studies to assess the market size and growth of the medical plastics market. The highlights from Grand View Research, Inc., on the market size and growth are

- The worldwide health-related plastics industry is expected to grow at a compound annual growth rate (CAGR) of 6.1 percent type between 2019–2025
- The global pharmaceutical unit sector created much more than USD300 billion in the year 2015.
- Devices and equipment applications accounted for over half of the global medical polymers market size in 2019 and projects more than 8 percent CAGR up to 2024.

According to Transparency Market Research, the medical-related plastics business size will grow from USD22.8 billion in 2019 to USD31.7 billion by 2024, at a CAGR of 6.8 percent.

A report issued by Polaris Market Research claims the global health-related plastics marketplace will represent over USD37.5 billion by 2026. The global health-related plastics marketplace has an estimated CAGR of 6.1 percent.

According to World Market Research, the global Medical Plastics Market size has a value of USD33.6 billion by 2025.[1] It is likely to rise at a decent CAGR of more than 6 percent through 2024. The US accounted for close to a 45-percent share of the entire pharmaceutical unit of the company in 2015, with over 6,500 pharmaceutical unit manufacturing businesses. Table 1.1 summarizes these findings:

**Table 1.1    Review of Studies on Medical Plastics Market**

| | *Market Size* | *Forecast* | *Market Size* | *Market Growth* |
|---|---|---|---|---|
| Grand View Research | USD22.26 billion in 2018 | $33.6 billion by 2025 | | CAGR of 6.1 percent from the year 2019 to 2025 |
| Transparency Market Research | USD22.8 billion in 2019 | USD31.7 billion by 2024 | | CAGR of 6.8 percent |
| Polaris Market Research | | USD37.5 billion by 2026 | | CAGR of 6.1 percent. |
| World Market Research | | USD33.6 billion by 2025 | | CAGR 6 percent up to 2025 |

# Note

1. https://worldmarketsresearch.weebly.com/blog/category/medical-devices

*Chapter 2*

# Growth of the Medical Plastics Market

## Product Differentiation Based on Design

Several factors have an impact on medical plastic products. These factors greatly influence the outcomes and their commercialization strategy in the various distribution channels. Competition in the medical plastics market is based on product differentiation with factors such as the following:

- design differentiation
- multiple functionalities, technical performance
- sustainable development

In the field of medical plastics, product differentiation could be classified according to several criteria. There is a market impact and an internal impact (costs and supply chain).

DOI: 10.4324/9781003212898-2

## A Differentiation Based on Processes and Materials

The different plastic processes in medical devices could also be differentiated based on methods and materials. They are classified into four different segments:

- polypropylene (syringe, laboratory equipment, medical bags)
- polyethylene (syringe plunger, laboratory equipment, medical kit, administrative apparatus)
- PVC (catheter, medical bag, administrative device)
- plastic engineering products (surgical equipment, sterilization tray, implant, residential medical device)

### DESIGN AND PERFORMANCE OF MEDICAL DEVICES ACCORDING TO DUPONT

DuPont, a multinational company, has become a significant player in the production of thermoplastic polymers. Its various skills include materials research, application development, and technical support for compliance analysis. DuPont differentiates its products by quality based on these processes:

- manufacturing according to GMP principles
- control of content contact during packaging
- data analsyis on sterilization methods

For example, DuPont has promoted Tyvek®, a durable material that helps a wide variety of industries, including medicine.

*Source*: DuPont promotion material

Plastic gathers several market segments and products by category with significant growth.

## Growth in Clinic Accessories

The clinic accessories segment creates a need for healthcare polymers to generate syringes, catheters, blood bags, and pharmaceutical pots. These polymers led to opportunities in hospital accessories as light, corrosion-resistant, and sterilized materials.

Health-related biopolymers are also appropriate for different sterilizing techniques like vaporized stream and hydrogen peroxide, gamma radiations, and ethylene oxide, making it probably the most suitable choice for the healthcare market.

This segment shows considerable development and is forecasted to attain a market value of USD3.44 billion by 2021.

## Growth in Analysis Systems

Health-related polymers are popular in the examination as reagents or perhaps as enhancers. They significantly improve the functionality of the test substances. Medical polymers offer sound support to bind the supplies that help in more straightforward detection and isolation, thus, establishing themselves as an essential component of in-vitro analytical methods. The most often used polymeric substances in this segment are polydimethylsiloxane, polycarbonate, polymethyl methacrylate, cyclo-olefin polymer, and polystyrene.

Growth in this segment is estimated to reach a CAGR of 6 percent by 2025.

## Growth in Medical Devices

The medical device market continues to develop together with most of the global healthcare market. This market represents as much as a 60 billion dollars-a-year-market in the United States and over 1,150 billion dollars worldwide.

Many emerging trends play a vital role in the market of medical plastics. The list includes improvements in substances that offer increased performance, making companies push product design structure. Upgrading and implementing new methods helps treat different diseases. The acceptance of requirements, coupled with an expanding volume of the medical, clinic, and outpatient methods, is projected to expand.

## Healthcare Polymer Market Growth

Healthcare polymer market products include medical-related fibers and resins, biodegradable medical plastics, and medical elastomers. Fibers, as well as resins, are polyvinyl chloride (PVC), polypropylene (PP), polyethylene (PE), and polystyrene (other thermoplastics).

This segment produced more than USD8 billion for the worldwide health-related polymers marketplace in 2015. It can develop at more than an 8-percent CAGR on account of innovative technologies to tweak implant abilities and enhance biocompatibility.

## Market Growth of Polypropylene

Polypropylene emerged as the fastest-growing plastic for medical packaging. Grand View Reports estimates a 9.2 percent CAGR for the material by 2025. The report noted an increase in the manufacture of top-quality plastic composites for specific applications to attain a high degree of product distinction.

## Growth for Polymer Engineering

Among the innovative materials in medical plastics, there are products associated with polymer engineering. The main applications of engineering polymers are medical devices and products.

The global market value for engineering plastics was estimated to be USD90 billion in the US in 2020. The growing size of this market is due to the increasing demand for innovative materials.

## Growth in Medical Packaging

Medical packaging manufacturing is growing at a continued rate, as ecological packaging films are being introduced that fight against the dangerous conditions that the contents and packaging are exposed to, including humidity, the supply chain, microbes and contaminants, heat and cold, and water.

Medical polymer films and barrier packaging protect products from exposure to ambient conditions, including stress, magnetic fields, vibration, and compression.

Polystyrene is a widespread material owing to its light weight, versatility, insulating properties, stability, and low cost. Extended polystyrene (EPS) strengthens reliability and wards off contamination. EPS is non-toxic, as it is made with only 2 percent material and is composed of 98 percent air.

## Growth in Plastic Bags

The international medical plastics market's total worth is slated to reach new heights in the years to follow. However, despite the growing significance of medical plastics, with plastic bags within healthcare, the market could be affected by growing criticism of non-biodegradable products.

Medical waste contributes to environmental pollution, and the industry is under constant scrutiny from government authorities and state bodies. However, the healthcare industry's efforts toward the proper disposal of wastes are a sound strategy for development and are becoming more critical for buyers. Therefore, the global medical plastics market could thrive due to resilience and the seriousness shown by healthcare bodies toward waste disposal.

The uses of plastics inside the healthcare industry have an assortment of aspects. The utilization of plastic bags is a fundamental necessity across medical operations and ward theatres. Moreover, the demand for storing precise surgical instruments is met through plastic container boxes.

The necessity for security in the healthcare industry has resulted in growth for plastic bags. Even with the pressure to recycle plastic bags, we can estimate that this segment's growth remains above 4 percent.

## Growth in Injection Molding and Medical Packaging

The lion's share of medical plastics' growth is in injection molding, in which precision areas are created and used for items like surgical catheters and syringes. Tubing extruders make essential components for drug delivery as well as fluid handling.

Sheet extruders make products that are contained in fluid-handling applications in addition to medical gowns and bedding.

Blow molding is utilized to make products like components and vials for medical beds and other healthcare and hospital furniture. In terms of injection molding, the task economically turns out many forms, even those with complicated geometries. As an outcome, injection molding has displaced metal in a broad range of uses in which the high cost of metal fabrication is prohibitive.

Likewise, the expense is a critical development driver fueling the change to products that contain far more plastics, as producers feel pressure to minimize instrumentation price. Injection molding is causing a push toward higher volumes that favor plastic-made mass-production strategies rather than the usual design based on metals.

## Growth in Demand for Disposable (Syringes, Surgical Device)

Demand for plastics in disposable medical products such as syringes, gloves, surgical device components, and catheter tubing is likely to be get-up-and-go segment growth at a CAGR of 6.9 percent revenue by 2025. The demand for disposable medical products is rising sharply. Here are some findings:

■ The total value of disposable medical products is expected to grow from USD6.12 billion in 2005 to USD18.4 billion in 2025.
■ The estimated annual CAGR growth rate over the period 2003–2023 is 5.66 percent.
■ Since 2003, plastic resins have dominated disposable medical products and are expected to maintain their position until 2023.

## Growth of Transparent Plastic Products

Manufacturers are developing new innovative products such as transparent plastic products for the medical market. These products must be more reliable and more efficient product with reduced costs.

Examples of innovative improvements through new combinations include reducing noise and vibration, absence of bisphenol A, deficiency of antimicrobial agents, and new sterilization methods. Additional examples include other liquid injection molding processes, liquid silicone rubber, urethane, and casting molds.

Plastic manufacturers are also introducing new products and developing recent trends to support this market's ambient growth. Plastic manufacturers are also introducing new products and developing recent trends to support this market's ambient growth—one of the trends in the manufacture of colorless products by combining materials. The benefits of transparent products include facilitating inspections, joining tubes with flexibility and performance, and increasing process accuracy.

The marketplace for transparent plastics is principally driven by the increasing need for plastics from the product packaging business, mainly from the packaging sector. This particular need derives from plastic's anti-microorganism, moisture barrier, and corrosion-resistant nature. These advantages offer a heightened shelf life to food items.

Transparent plastics are commonly used in the pharmaceutical and FMCG packaging business and are expected to grow in the marketplace in the coming years. Furthermore, the use of these FMCG packaging in electric cars is increasing due to their secured insulation qualities and mechanical properties. Therefore, several product developments may also enjoy a significant beneficial effect from the transparent plastics market development. From the green point of view, the burgeoning expansion of electric vehicles worldwide is a crucial element in pushing the marketplace.

According to a new account by Reports and Data, the transparent plastics market is expected to reach USD159.82 billion by 2026. The marketplace for plastic in the North American region accounts for the second-largest share (27.3 percent) of the market in 2018. The presence of prominent organized players in this region contributes to this large percentage. These organizations are focusing their efforts on staying in line with market trends.

According to BCC Research, the North American market for rigid transparent plastics should rise from 4.7 billion pounds by size in 2018 to 6.1 billion pounds in 2023, at a CAGR of 5.2 percent from 2018 through 2023.

## Growth of the 3-D Printing Plastics

The integration of various industry factors has contributed to the expansion of the plastics market. Among the notable

aspects in this respect is improving federal initiatives for supporting the incorporation of 3-D printing plastics in several
different industries. These national initiatives have generated
multiple uses and the establishment of 3-D printing plastics
involving various end-user industries such as the healthcare
market and the automobile sector, which have a positive effect
on industry development.

The global 3D printing plastics market size is expected to
reach USD2.83 billion by 2027, according to a new study by
Grand View Research, Inc. The market is projected to register
a substantial CAGR of 23.7% during the forecast period, due to
rising demand from various end-use industries such as medical, automotive, aerospace and defense, and consumer goods.[1]

According to Reports and Data, the 3-D printing plastics
market will reach USD3,143.1 million by 2026.

■ The 3-D printing plastics market size was evaluated at
  USD611.8 million in 2018 a CAGR of 21.2 percent.
■ The 3-D printing plastics industry is predicted to experience significant development throughout the forecasted
  period.

Table 2.1 summarizes these findings:

**Table 2.1   Global 3D printing plastics**

|  | Market Size | Forecast | Market Growth (CAGR) |
|---|---|---|---|
| Grand View Research |  |  | 24.9% through 2025 |
| Market and Markets | USD9.9 billion in 2018 | USD34.8 billion by 2024 |  |
| StratView Research |  |  | 28.2% through 2025 |
| Reports and Data |  |  | 21.2% |

## Growth for 3-D Printing

3-D printing technology helps medical device companies and pharmaceutical companies create treatment-specific medications and patient-specific implants and allows surgeons novel resources for preparing methods. The technology is moving toward 4-D printing, which could be defined as the action or process of using 3-D printing techniques to create an object that can predictably change its shape or properties over time in response to conditions such as contact with heat, water, air, or an electric current. This technology includes a time dimension and energy source.

### Adoption of 4-D Printing and New Opportunities

The adoption of 4-D printing is imminent, as it helps the improvement of sensible substances. State-of-the-art 4-D printing programs reportedly can transform their color, shape, and properties, reduce manufacturing time, and lower post-processing needs.

Both 4-D and 3-D printing improve understanding of disease states and the refined patient-specific look of implantable products and surgical tools.

## Growth for Medical Imaging Products and Other Disposable Medical Products

The demand for plastic products in the medical and dental field is mainly for medical imaging products and disposable medical products. This is the third-most important segment. They are ranked in importance of the order of disposable medical products, medical devices, and products for image diagnostics. Medical consumables represent 21.9 percent of the market, and imaging products 35.8 percent.

The three main sectors represent 79.2 percent of the plastics market in the medical and dental fields.

## Growth of Plastics in Dentistry[2]

The field of dentistry has emerged as a profitable area within medicine. The masses spend a substantial part of their income on dental treatment, which offers several medical manufacturers new opportunities. Medical plastics to develop dentures and dental cement storage have played a dynamic role in the global market's growth.

### Dental 3-D Printing Market

According to Market and Markets, the dental 3-D printing market was valued at 1.39 billion in 2017. The dental 3D Printing market is likely to grow at a CAGR of 23.2 percent to reach USD5.06 billion by 2023.

# Growth of Medical Plastics by Geographic Market

Geographically, Asia-Pacific accounted for approximately 24.5 percent of global revenue in 2016, driven by progress in consumer healthcare spending, tied with high medical tourism levels, primarily in China and India.

## The United States

The market for medical devices is a significant contributor to the advancement in the medical plastics market. The international market for medical devices is large, fragmented, and relatively complex to circumscribe.

This market's total value reaches USD140 billion, with a dominance in the United States and Europe.

The US accounted for close to 45 percent of the entire pharmaceutical unit company in 2015 with over 6,500 pharmaceutical unit manufacturing businesses.[3]

Increased healthcare expenditure by the population on account of growing incidences of lifestyle illnesses and ailments in North America is likely to drive the medical plastics market growth. The region is expected to register a CAGR of 6.3 percent from 2019 to 2025. The increase is determined by the rise in demand for such devices, generic drugs, and healthcare services.

Regarding the exports from the United States to its main partners, those linked to the health sector have received between 10 percent and 20 percent of the total US exports, and the numbers are increasing. It is possible for the companies operating in the plastics processing industry to target these export markets, which are the most profitable.

## International Markets for Medical Plastics

In the international market, there are more than 8,500 types of medical devices. Technological innovation in the medical field extends lives and improves the quality of life of the patients. It leads to cost reductions and improvements in the health system. Several geographic markets are growing.

## Mexico and Canada

For instance, there is a speedy growth of the medicinal industry in Mexico and Canada. This is a favorable condition and expected to positively influence market development, mainly because of the subsequent pharmacological packaging demand. The demand for disposables is growing due to the rising cases of the occurrence of diseases. It is obvious to drive the regional market for medical plastics.

## Europe

There is also a growth in several European market segments. For example, there is rising adoption of dental and body contouring implants in Europe that is expected to have a positive impact on market progress over the estimated period. Increasing non-refundable income and rising cosmetic dentistry adoption are forecasted to propel the forecast period's regional product demand.

However, while Europe's healthcare-related polymers sector will steadily develop at under 7 percent CAGR through 2024, Asia Pacific, Latin America, the Middle East, and Africa will be observing a top development in the coming years.

## Asia

The Asian market, with 18 percent of the market share, is experiencing the most vigorous growth. China's market is witnessing substantial growth over the forecast period, which can be attributed to high healthcare costs, increasing private and public healthcare expenditure, and increased disease prevalence. The increasing elderly population in the country is a significant contributor to growth.

Improved healthcare initiatives in countries like China, Indonesia, Bangladesh, India, and Pakistan support market development in the Asia Pacific with an expected growth above 10 percent CAGR until 2025.

## The Middle East and West Africa

Growth can be found in the Middle East and West Africa. These markets are likely to be motivated by the call for medical components such as disposable gloves, catheters, and syringes. The market rise is due to the growing preference for high-grade medical facilities by the inhabitants in the middle- and lower-income-group consumers.

## Notes

1. https://www.grandviewresearch.com/industry-analysis/ medical-3d-printing-plastics-market.
2. Advancements in Dentistry. Browse Press Release. www. transparencymarketresearch.com/pressrelease/medical plastics market.htm.
3. https://www.gminsights.com/pressrelease/ medical-polymers-market.

*Chapter 3*

# Strategic Context of the Medical Plastics Market

In this section, we analyze the business context and the different environments of the medical plastics market. Our objective is to identify opportunities with a leverage effect on market development by strategically opening windows of possibilities. It also aims to identify challenges that could disrupt a company's cash flow in this sector.

The Strategic Context Index (SC Index) is a tool that provided an analysis of the opportunities and threats of the medical plastics market's strategic context. This section is based on PESTEL (political, economic, social, technological, environmental, and legal) analysis and perhaps an instrument utilized to analyze and keep track of the macro-environmental elements. The macro-environmental details might have a profound effect on an organization's efficiency.

Our SC Index for the medical plastics market shows that the context received an overall score of 74.5 percent, which is very good (Figure 3.1).

DOI: 10.4324/9781003212898-3

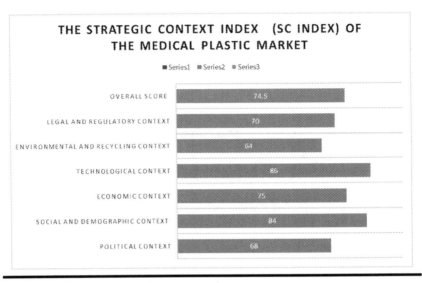

Figure 3.1    **Strategic context index (SC Index) for the medical plastics market.**

# Political Context

## *Challenges*

The most critical factor in the political context is the political pressure for all plastic products until 2025. The tensions on health facilities in hospitals for the disposal of plastic products were massive and could disrupt the design of the production and distribution of medical products and plastics.

As we shall see in more detail, this political pressure on the market for medical plastics introduces a new plastic economy.

## *The New Plastic Economy*

The Ellen MacArthur Foundation presents a set of arguments in favor of what has been called the New Plastic Economy. The following topics are part of the arguments raised by the foundation.

Plastics have grown to be the essential substance of the contemporary economic climate. It has the strength of combining unrivaled and functional qualities at a low cost. The use of plastic has improved 20-fold in the past half-century. It is anticipated to double once again within the next 20 years.

Today, almost everyone everywhere encounters plastics on a daily basis. This report prominently emphasizes the "plastic-packaging." While delivering many benefits, today's plastics economy has drawbacks that are starting to be more evident by the day. After a brief first use cycle, 95 percent of plastic packaging material, worth maybe USD80 billion to USD120 billion annually, is sacrificed in the economic system.

The economy is supported by and lined up with concepts of the rounded economy. The drive is to distribute better system-wide economic and green outcomes by building a helpful after-use plastics economy, radically lowering the outflow of plastics into natural methods (the ocean) and other harmful externalities and decoupling from fossil feedstocks.

Several factors explain the growth of the new plastic economy:

- Radically upsurge the economics, quality, and uptake of recycling.
- Scale up the adoption of reusable packaging.
- Scale up the implementation of industrially compostable plastic packaging for targeted applications.

The new plastic economic system's perspective is that plastics should never become waste and disposable materials reenter the economy with new usages. A staggering 32 percent of transparent plastic packaging escapes collection methods, generating considerable economic costs by decreasing the output of essential organic methods like the ocean and clogging urbanized infrastructure.

# Social and Demographic Context

## *Opportunity*

If we look at trends in the social and demographic context, a definite pattern in the opportunities is presented by the aging population until 2025. This is a strong trend as the aging population is associated with higher consumption of health services products. It generates demand in the home, clinical, and hospital care market.

## *Innovative Health Products for the Aging Population*

As we discussed before, the population's aging represents an extensive opportunity for the medical plastics market.

Moreover, a rise in changing lifestyle and disposable income, increasing innovative health solutions, and the need for efficient and affordable healthcare systems, like 3-D printed implants and personalized products, drive the industry. The main drivers for health plastics manufacturing include the necessity for advanced health equipment for the aging population.

The health plastics industry's main drivers also include the need for innovative health products for the aging population in emerging economies like India and China. According to the report, the health device industry is driven by worldwide population growth, owing to increased access for customers to healthcare services—especially in developing economies—and mounting replacement of metal parts in surgical apparatuses. Also, the development of advanced materials with improved strength and performance pushes the market forward.

A growing number of insured people in the US that carries with it a need for medical devices is anticipated to have a positive effect on the expansion with the forecast years. The marketplace is characterized by the existence of many businesses active in the generation of innovative grade plastics.

## Consumerization

Consumerization is the process of enterprise technology being changed or influenced by new technologies emerging from consumer markets into professional arenas. Certain types of smartphones, for example, began as a consumer product and are now used extensively in corporate environments, military contexts, and other professional spheres.

There continues to be a rise in the consumerization of medical products. Materials can provide a better flow to fill thin walls as well as have sophisticated capabilities so that designers can form lighter and smaller devices to yield a much better product.

"There is a push for healthcare in the house environment or even in a comfortable, convenient establishing instead of the doctor's office or maybe hospital," said Phil Katen, president of Erie, PA-based injection molder Plastics. "We are seeing far more gadgets being created that allow patients to follow a far more active lifestyle," he argues.[1]

The primary drivers—the growth of new technologies (e.g., social media and smartphones) increased focus on expenses, along with heightened buyer expectations—are prompting device companies to increase the commitment to theirs too and invest in improving patient empowering solutions that use certain information.

## A Growing Number of Insured People with Medical Devices

A growing number of insured people in the US come with the resultant need for medical devices that positively affects the forecast years' expansion.[2] The marketplace has several players active in generating innovative grade plastics to introduce in the market. We are discovering accelerated development in the healthcare field driven by the demographics of the baby boomers. It is they wish to lead a high quality of living and healthy life. The generation has a better understanding of healthcare than the former generations. It is very positive to see that medical devices and manufacturers of medical devices are assisting this generation by providing required medical care to live an active lifestyle. The plastic processors are inhibited by creating products like a pump, meant to provide convenience and better performance.

## Less Physically Intrusive Health Therapies

A medical procedure is described as non-invasive when no breaking in the skin is produced. And there is no exposure to the mucosa, or maybe skin break, or perhaps an internal body cavity beyond an artificial or natural body orifice. For instance, painful palpation and percussion are non-invasive, but a rectal examination is invasive. The failure to attend to the injuries related to the eardrum and nose is the failure of the non-invasive medical terms process.

Breakthroughs in healthcare science promise an assortment of less physically intrusive health therapies. This breakthrough may reduce the demand for disposable health devices mostly made up of plastics.

## Serving an Ecosystem with Different Stakeholders

From a social perspective, there is some complexity in serving the medical plastics ecosystem structured with stakeholders with different vested interests. You find specific competitors that create the most concern within any community—generally, those with the most significant market share. The value provided by medical plastics products could be analyzed by meeting the need of three stakeholders: the practice offering, the patient's needs, and the competitive offerings.

The model uses a Venn diagram-based analysis that facilitates an immediate comprehension of the practice's naturally competitive situation against an individual competitor for promoting medical plastics products. It leads to complex sales, additionally referred to as Enterprise product sales, which can easily relate to a technique of trading often worn by businesses when procuring big contracts for products or services in which the buyer takes command of the marketing activity by issuing a request for proposal (RFP) and also needs a proposal to reply out of earlier recognized or maybe engaged suppliers. Complex product sales include long sales cycles with many decision-makers. Several stakeholders, as well as stakeholder groups, help every complicated deal.

In the medical plastics market, numerous buyers or integrated stakeholders' importance pertains to the level of risks associated with the investment in products and services.

# Economic Context

## *Opportunities*

If the demand for medical expenses coverage comes from occurrences, companies facilitate the growth of the market. However, the economic and cycle-sensitive environment (like the after-COVID-19) economic context might lead to economic downturns. The economic and cycle-sensitive environment could disrupt discretionary revenues available to buyers by hospitals and health clinics to purchase plastic medical products until 2025. The COVID-19 accentuates this threat.

## *Reducing Medical Costs*

The integration of transparent plastic into modern medicine has slowly risen within the past ten years. Health-related plastics have considerably reduced medicine costs and pain management. The economic landscape may influence an R&D investment decision.

Vulnerability: An additional challenge is an absence of funding for start-up or small businesses that are especially vulnerable to reduced venture capital difficulty. This absence of financing could adversely affect the broader market by limiting innovation and growth.

## Disposable Income

Additionally, an increase in disposable income, changing lifestyle, need for efficient and affordable healthcare systems, increasing use of innovative health solutions, like 3-D printed implants and personalized products, drive the industry.

## Recession Proof

Unlike automotive or various other end markets, the healthcare industry includes consistent growth of approximately 3 to 5 percent a year. Additionally, it is relatively recession proof.

## Fluctuation in Oil Prices

Fluctuation in oil prices is a significant component accountable for volatile charges of Polyvinyl Chloride (PVC), Polyethylene (PE), Polypropylene (PP), and polystyrene. Contraction and capacity expansion also contribute to cost volatility. Additionally, rising overproduction in the Chinese market is anticipated to affect the raw material rates.

# Technological Context

## Opportunities

Overall, the technological context represents an indispensable opportunity since trends such as miniaturization and the introduction of technologies entered production. The product connectivity, particularly in wearables and the Internet of Things, represents a strategic opportunity for market development for medical plastics manufacturers until 2025.

## Technological Evolution

Resources combined with emerging technologies are critical drivers for the development of the sector.

According to Peter Galland, the business supervisor of PVC medical-related compounds for Teknor, Apex Company. Teknor has probably demonstrated the most reliable pattern in disposable vinyl medical-related plastics replacement DEHP along with other ortho phthalate plasticizers with acceptable and affordable alternatives.

Unlike automotive or various other end markets, the healthcare industry includes consistent growth of approximately 3 to 5 percent a year. Additionally, it is relatively recession proof.

Corporations resort to innovative product developments as one of the main strategies to attain market growth. Also, key market players capitalize significantly on R&D to develop advanced products.

However, the medical plastics market is subject to technological advancements in producing advanced plastics for healthcare applications.

## Considerable Technological Evolution

The considerable evolution of technologies in the medical plastics market represents a significant opportunity for market development. For instance, the healthcare plastic market techniques have recently undergone significant changes, with conventional to advanced polymers.

The increasing trend of new technologies, such as polycarbonate-based healthcare plastic, is finding a considerable opportunity for disposables, catheters, and medical instrument programs, due to consistent qualities for dependable functionality and clarity as UV transparency and much better heat resistance.

The disposables use different technologies such as acrylics, polyurethane, polycarbonate, polyester, polystyrene, polypropylene, polyethylene, and polyvinyl chloride-based healthcare plastic technologies utilized in implants, medical bags, surgical instruments, catheters, and drug delivery method applications. Increasing use of sterilized and disposable equipment and demand for medical products' longer shelf life produce brand new possibilities for various healthcare plastic solutions.

## Technology as a Driver of Innovation

According to *Plastic News*, innovation continues to drive development in the medical sector from synthetic bones to replacement heart valves, hospital beds to light treatments, and healthcare technology innovation's social and economic effects cannot be overstated.[3] Plastic-made continues to play a vital role in these segments.

Breakthroughs in healthcare science promise an assortment of less physically intrusive health therapies, which reduce the demand for disposable health devices, mostly made up of plastics. In the distant future, these forces, to some degree, counter the usually positive trajectory for using plastics in medical devices.

Improvements in polymers play an essential role in the medical device industry. Lately, supplies, for instance, polyolefins, have discovered increased utilization as substitutes for glass—vials.

For instance, in the orthopedic store, polyolefins provide many benefits, including DEHP, used in healthcare tubing, and the critical problem is to discover an alternate material. It represents a good substance profile and cost-effectiveness. They have found several uses in healthcare packaging, drug delivery equipment, and products like medical bowls. To fulfill this need, businesses like Borealis Healthcare are gaining ground, offering goods just for the healthcare industry.

Biobased resources produce a great deal of interest, but there is a reluctance to pay a high quality for them after comprehensive functionality tests and cost impact analysis.

## *Miniaturization*

Miniaturization is an important trend in medical plastics.[4] The primary drivers are the growth of new technologies (e.g., social media) and smartphones, increased focus on expenses, along heightened buyer expectations. They are prompting device companies to increase their investment and investment in improving patient empowering solutions that use particular info.

Style elements must ensure that the unit is movement-resistant and sweat, comfortable, waterproof, and meets health-and-safety-related needs.

In the case of miniaturized wearable devices, for instance, style elements must make sure that the unit is movement-resistant and sweat, comfortable, waterproof, and meets up with health-and-safety-related needs.

The primary drivers are—the growth of new technologies (e.g., social media) and smartphones, increased focus on expenses, and heightened buyer expectations. They are prompting device companies to increase the commitment to their apps and personally invest in improving patient empowering solutions that use certain information.

Mark Bonifacio, the co-founder of Bonifacio Consulting Services, observed that miniaturization is a distinctive pattern in the healthcare industry, and plastic processors are seizing on the chance it provides.

"We see a rise in home-based healthcare across hospitalization, and this is driving the need for miniaturization of healthcare devices," he explained. "As an outcome, we see an increasing need for precision, in addition to miniaturization of healthcare devices."[5]

## Biocompatibility as Well as Longevity

Biocompatibility and longevity have become the essential characteristics of raw materials utilized to produce healthcare plastic products. Metal replacement is also a continuing pattern in the healthcare room.

Single-use products are not as likely to result in healthcare-associated infections as recyclable instruments and must be sterilized after each use. Plastics offer radiolucency, allow light-weighting, and lower stress-shielding. As they are radiolucent, polymer-based medical gadgets permit surgeons to get an unobstructed view.

## Traceability

Traceability is still pushed, in significant part, by the scrutiny of the FDA and the compliant demands which the OEMs should guarantee are in position. The OEMs are showing interest in designing and producing new ranges only because they want to pass the approval and consulting process. Also, having traceability is the most significant factor of OEM.

Bonifacio argues that today's strong demand is cradle-to-grave traceability, and that is vitally important. "We are discovering new developments," he said. One point is a substance in which you put anything in a polymer. When a spectral light strikes it, it lets off a color. There is a great deal of promise. He argues:

> Peter Galland of Teknor also highlights that traceability must be a key focus. The chance of any post-shipment queries coming from the area is low. However, the possible impact of risk is rather high. This particular kind of accountability is a

foundational component of virtually any materials partnership with clients and suppliers.[6]

## Traceability and Sensors

The MRP structure in this procedure is becoming crucial. All too often, lots of healthcare manufacturers fail to know that. It is not about having systems that are different but how you archive all the information from engineering drawings, inspection reports, SOP reports, and tools. All this must be managed in one file. The ERP and MRP-like devices are handy to keep information readily available and most used since 2017.

Traceability could draw from some other fields like military explosives and devices. "We have extended the discussed and developing identifiers into transparent plastic a lot as they do in the explosive industry," Len Czuba, the President of Czuba Enterprises Inc., said. Nobody has discovered the right solution to this. It is excellent news to know identifiers on each used unit. It should be a design that does not modify a function and change the look of a device.

## The Case of Lucintel

Lucintel analysis finds that healthcare plastic engineering is forecasted to develop at 5 percent during the next five years. Polyvinylchloride is the most significant part of this industry, and it is growing at above-average development. GW Plastics, Baxter International, Cyro Industries, Dickinson and Becton, Medplast, Freudenberg Medical, Du Pont, ExxonMobil Corporation, Dow, DuPont, plus Rochling Group are among the leading players in the healthcare plastic industry.

The Lucintel statement can catalyze development since it offers extensive analysis and data on fashion, key drivers, and instructions. The report contains strategic implications, forecasts, trends, disruption potential, regulatory compliance, competitive intensity, and technology readiness for the worldwide healthcare plastic engineering by material engineering program, as follows:

■ Engineering readiness by technology type
■ Regulatory compliance and competitive intensity

# Environmental and Recycling Context

## *Opportunities*

In the environmental context, as in the political context, buyers are looking for solutions for recycling and recovering medical plastics by 2025. The concept of sustainable development must be part of product design. Biodegradability and recycling opportunities have become an emergent attribute of plastic products.

## *Healthcare Plastic Recycling*

Globally, only 14 percent of plastic is collected for reprocessing, according to the Ellen MacArthur Foundation publication *The New Plastics Economy: Catalysing Action*. In the medical plastics market, the rate is even lower. The lack of worldwide standards and an intricate value chain has weakened healthcare plastics' awareness as a feasible recycling feedstock.

Nevertheless, for innovative and entrepreneurial recyclers, the healthcare industry represents one of the last untapped sources of high-quality recyclable plastics. If you ever have spent somewhat time in a hospital, you probably notice the medical material thrown into the trashed bin. The product includes gowns, irrigation bottles, IV bags, pitchers, trays, sterilization wrap, and packaging material. Almost all the products are used once and then disposed of.

According to a study published by *Slate*, US hospitals cause 6 million tons of waste annually, with plastics accounting for up to one-quarter of that whole. Most of that plastic winds up in landfills or incinerators though 85 percent of it is non-hazardous and free from patient contact and contamination.

## Replacement of DEHP

According to Peter Galland, the business supervisor of PVC medical-related compounds for Teknor Apex Co, probably the most reliable pattern in disposable vinyl medical-related plastics is the replacement of DEHP with other ortho phthalate plasticizers with acceptable, affordable alternatives. DEHP: A softener for (PVC) polyvinyl chloride, a plastic polymer, is used in various products. Unplasticized PVC is rigid and stiff at room temperature. A plasticizer (softener) is added to raise the elasticity of the polymer. DEHP is the plasticizer for leading PVC medical equipment and devices.

The list of the devices includes DEHP-plasticized PVC blood bags and infusion tubing, nasogastric tubes, umbilical artery catheters, intravenous (IV) bags and tubing, enteral nutrition feeding bags, peritoneal dialysis bags and tubing, pipes used in extracorporeal membrane oxygenation (ECMO), tubing used in cardiopulmonary bypass (CPB) procedures, and tubing used during hemodialysis.

## Alternative to DEHP

DEHP is the plasticizer for maximum PVC healthcare devices. A plasticizer (softener) is added to raise the elasticity of the polymer. Until 2010, diethyl hexyl phthalate (DEHP) was the plasticizer most often accustomed to file down PVC health devices (MDs) due to an excellent efficiency/cost ratio. For elastic plasticized PVC, phthalates usually are not chemically bound to PVC, and they are introduced worldwide and, therefore, can come in touch with individuals.

The European Directive 2007/47/CE classified DEHP as a scanner and toxicity danger and restricted its use in MDs. MD producers were thus driven to immediately find DEHP alternatives to keep PVC nutrition tubing's suppleness, infusion sets, and hemodialysis lines.

Many replacement plasticizers, the so-called alternative to DEHP plasticizers, had been integrated into the MDs. Today, the danger of contact with these ingredients for hospitalized patients, especially in cases categorized at-risk, hasn't yet been examined. This is because migration research, supplying adequate coverage and man toxicity information, hasn't been performed.

# Legal and Regulatory Context

## Moderate Threat

A moderate threat introduces a regulatory framework for plastic products concerning biodegradability from a legal and regulatory perspective. Generally, there is a trend toward the harmonization of regulatory frameworks. That might put pressure on medical plastics providers.

Organizational details of regulatory frameworks between the North American, European, and Asian markets might create mobility barriers to create new products. Regulations may also affect divestment for products that are not aligned with new regulatory standards. We think about the uprising environmental concern.

## Strict Regulations

Today's regulatory landscape: in California, Europe, and Washington State, DEHP plasticizes eight can't exceed 1,000 ppm by weight (0.1 percent) without requiring warning labels highlighting the existence of the deliberate use of DEHP or maybe the presence of DEHP as a contaminant.[7]

The governing companies in various states of the US have shown a heightened affinity toward plastic-made recycling.

Strict regulations are imposed by different health agencies, REACH, FDA, and WHO. The product quality and prices might also hinder the medical-related polymers market growth in the future years.[8] For instance, in Europe, medical products belong to the European Council Directive (93/42/EEC), which helps consume theirs. Restructuring of the European laws for this kind of product is anticipated to emerge as one of the primary key factors impacting regional growth.

## A Movement toward Stricter Compliance

New emerging trends feature more strict compliance, driven by the OEMs and determined by the FDA. Uncertainty looms as government works with Congress to define the Affordable Care Act's world.

If the ACA is repealed and an additional program replaces it, significant adjustments in the funding and provisions of healthcare will likely have renewed focus on cutting down expenses in all levels of the medical care market such as the medical device tax.

## Developing a Method for DEHP Alternatives

*Plastic News* says DEHP alternatives be the number-one regulatory problem for medical device-makers in developing a DEHP alternatives method. However, the issues around scientific interpretation and consumer perception drive a more in-depth investigation into many available plasticizer alternatives and trade-offs. Many OEMs have mostly switched to substitute plasticizers by now.

DEHP is a softener for polyvinyl chloride (PVC), a plastic polymer used in a wide array of products. Un-plasticized PVC is hard and brittle at room temperature.

## Medical Products and the EC Directives

In Europe, medical products belong to the European Council Directive (93/42/EEC), which consumes theirs.[9] Restructuring of the European laws for this kind of product is anticipated to emerge as one of the primary key factors impacting regional growth. The governing companies in various states of the US have shown a heightened affinity toward plastic-made recycling.

In Europe, medical products belong to the European Council Directive (93/42/EEC), which consumes theirs. Restructuring of the European laws for this kind of product is anticipated to emerge as one of the primary key factors impacting regional growth.

In the US, the federal agencies in the nation expended an entire of USD35.9 billion in healthcare R&D in 2015, in a move likely to offer impetus to the development of the healthcare sector, translating into the expansion of the health plastics market. For example, polyether-ether-ketone (PEEK), a high-performance biocompatible material, has made many strides in several medicinal applications. Evonik recently publicized that its Vestakeep-branded PEEK polymer exists in more than 80 medical devices transparent by the FDA.

## Counterfeiting

### Using Authentication

Driven by counterfeiting, outsourced manufacturing, plus rising warranty expenses, OEMs are compounds to covertly "fingerprint" the products of theirs in the margin that is high and substantial responsibility marketplaces.

Counterfeiting has impacted a broad range of things, from folding bicycles to snow jackets to health items, including glucose test strips. The counterfeit test strips evolved into a safety concern when patients used their results to establish just how much insulin they required. Typical trace and track strategies include overt tools like inks, labels, laser marking, or maybe holograms, but these occasionally provide minimal shelter since counterfeiters could duplicate them.

## Counterfeiting Proactive Strategies

Track-and-trace methods utilizing alphanumeric barcodes permit information to be collected from each step in the supply chain, enhancing security, taxation, and healthcare compensation. It can likewise supply a higher level of transparency for individuals, who could find out the story of their specific medicine by scanning a package's QR code with their smartphone.

In-line serialization helps you guarantee component security by boosting traceability and compliance with the Food and Drug Administrations.

Covert track and trace strategies include methods like energy-sensitive or micro-printed taggants. Forensic trace and track techniques could go even more deeply into the content itself.

Optical dyes and pigments are utilized to discreetly differentiate between 2 products, which might appear the same under regular lighting problems but have different colors under specific light wavelengths.

## *The Case of APLIX Self-Gripping Fasteners*

Headquartered in Charlotte, NC, APLIX is among the world's top hook and loop fastening method specialists. To serve the aircraft, automotive, cleaning, healthcare, personal attention, wrapping, and other particular industries, APLIX is mainly active in the United States, with offices in Brazil, France, and China.

Standard fasteners from APLIX meet the specifications of several applications in the healthcare industry. Custom finished items molded by APLIX could deal with the project from concept to production, and inserts created and made by APLIX, which are mounted to the injection mold by way of a license agreement.

The functions of APLIX self-gripping fasteners are assembling, fixing, and joining. Over one billion meters of loop and hook is produced every year. Many of our products are custom-made to meet exact needs and applications—the growth and development of APLIX through our clients' accomplishments. The advanced manufacturing department, experienced research team, dedicated sales force, and suppliers' ingenuity are the crucial factors in APLIX's progress and make it a solution for every fastening need. The advantages are appearance, elimination of adhesive-backed hook tape, add-on labor, and chemical and liquid resistance by APLIX.

## Notes

1. https://www.plasticsnews.com/article/20100125/ NEWS/301259975/katen-philip-a.
2. https://www.plasticsnews.com/article/20100125/ NEWS/301259975/katen-philip-a.
3. https://www.plasticsnews.com/article/20100125/ NEWS/301259975/katen-philip-a.
4. https://www.plasticsnews.com/article/20100125/ NEWS/301259975/katen-philip-a.
5. https://www.medicaldesignandoutsourcing. com/7-trends-made-medtech-manufacturing-today/.
6. https://www.medicalplasticsnews.com/topics/peter-galland/.
7. file:///C:/Users/sabourin_v/Downloads/PN_20190812_1%20(4).pdf.
8. https://www.ncbi.nlm.nih.gov/pmc/articles/PMC3791860/
9. http://crowaptukend.gotdns.ch/forum/?q=plastics+in+medical+devices+properties+requirements+and+applications+by+vinny+r.+sastri

*Chapter 4*

# Factors Determining Growth of the Plastics Market

The health plastics industry's main drivers include the need for innovative health products from the aging population and increasing healthcare investments in emerging economies like India and China.

We found six factors that are determining growth in the medical plastics market:

1. the growth of the polymers as functional substitutes
2. the aging of the population
3. the rising middle class in emergent markets,
4. the pervasiveness of cardiovascular problems and other diseases
5. low cost and biocompatibility of medical polymers
6. the applications in the diagnostic system, biodegradable hospital accessories, and implants

DOI: 10.4324/9781003212898-4

# Factor 1: The Growth of Polymers as Functional Substitutes

## Polymers Are Rapidly Changing Different Substances

Polymers are rapidly changing different substances like alloys, metals, and ceramics in different implants and developing industry dominance.[1] Polymer substances tend to be more flexible and may be used appropriately in uses like liver parts, kidneys, heart components, facial prostheses, tracheal tubes, dentures, and hip as well as knee joints.

## Improve the Functionality of the Test Substances

Health-related polymers are popular in the examination as reagents or perhaps as enhancers, as they significantly improve the test substances' functionality. Medical polymers offer sound support to bind the supplies that help in more straightforward detection and isolation, therefore establishing themselves as an essential component of in-vitro analytical methods. The most often used polymeric substances in this segment are polydimethylsiloxane, polycarbonate, polymethyl methacrylate, cyclo-olefin polymer, then polystyrene.

## PVC Allows Uninterrupted Monitoring of Substance Flow

The transparency of plasticized PVC allows uninterrupted monitoring of substance flow. PVC is sought for pharmaceutical, medical, and drug delivery applications due to its cost-efficiency and unique performance attributes.

PVC experience sustained demand in the decades to come despite concerns raised in certain quarters regarding its potential impact on human health. The transparency of plasticized

PVC allows uninterrupted monitoring of substance flow. PVC is sought for pharmaceutical, medical, and drug delivery applications due to its cost-efficiency and unique performance attributes. You find much more than 300 kinds of plasticizers, a maximum of hundreds of business use. Phthalate plasticizers found in several PVC-based items include life-saving medical devices like medical tubing and blood bags. Several experiments propose that DEHP phthalate might leach from medical devices made of flexible PVC. However, the results are much from conclusive in the terminology of the effect this might have on human health.

Nevertheless, the perceived downside might slightly affect the need for PVC solutions. Due to its multiple usages, PVC is poised to play a significant role in the increasing interest in medical fibers and resins. The resins and texture are part of the health polymers industry and develop over eight percent in a compound annual price through 2024.

Nevertheless, the perceived downside might slightly affect the need for PVC solutions. PVC prevails; however, the content is poised to play a noteworthy part in the increasing interest in medical fibers and resins due to the multiple benefits. As a situation of fact, the medical fibers and resins part of the health polymers industry developed over eight percent in a compound annual price through 2024.

## Proliferation of Plasticizers

There are more than three hundred kinds of plasticizers. A maximum of hundreds of that is in business use—phthalate plasticizers in several PVC-based items, including life-saving medical devices like medical tubing and blood bags. Several experiments propose that DEHP phthalate might leach from medical devices made of flexible PVC. However, the results are much from conclusive in the terminology of the effect this might have on human health.

## Medical-Grade Polymers for Surgical Instruments

Medical-grade polymers are a crucial part of the worldwide healthcare ecosystem. From surgical instruments to catheters and implants, polymers are found in an array of products.

## PEEK Polymers

PEEK polymers are not pretentious by lipids or blood—most of the diluters and enzymes in the body—and therefore have become broadly used in long-term orthopedic implant applications, including suture screws, plates and pins, and tissue anchors. PEEK is substituting metal as a hip stem component, as this polymer is more well-matched with the flexibility of natural bones than titanium or steel.

## Combating Harmful Conditions in the Supply Chain

Medical packaging is geared for sustained growth as ecological packaging films are being introduced that fight the adverse conditions the packaging and contents are exposed to heat and cold, in the supply chain, microbes, and contaminants, including humidity and water. Medical polymer barrier and film packaging shield products from revelation to ambient conditions and guard them against stress, vibration, magnetic fields, and compression. Polystyrene is a popular material owing to its lightweight, stability, insulating properties, and low cost. Expanded polystyrene (EPS) reinforces versatility and reliability and wards off contamination. EPS is non-toxic, as it is made with merely 2 percent material and is composed of 98 percent air.

# Factor 2: Aging of the Population

## Increasing Elderly Population

Increasing the elderly population and boosting healthcare demand among them may also guide the health polymers industry. The worldwide population of those more than 65 years of age grew to nearly 80 million between 2010 and 2015. Currently, this population represents over 8 percent of the total global population.

A complementary factor is the growing house-based health-care demand. Growing house-based healthcare demand likewise improves the global health-related polymers market in the future years. The increasing elderly population and life expectancy acquire this development and quickly spread chronic illnesses, technological advances, affordable house healthcare systems with alternate therapy techniques, and government initiatives related to the cause.

## Factor 3: Rising Middle Class in Emerging Markets

A growing middle class in emerging markets such as India, China, and Brazil assumes quality healthcare comparable to Western markets, and a continuing trend is favoring disposables. Polymer-based single-use devices are contributing to this growth.[2]

The health plastics industry's main drivers include the need for innovative health products from the aging population and increasing healthcare investments in emerging economies like India and China.[3]

## Factor 4: Pervasiveness of Cardiovascular Problems and Other Diseases

The medical polymer market progresses with the growing category of pharmaceutical devices. The omnipresence of cardiovascular issues, infections, general medical conditions, and other diseases coupled with the swelling development of procedures and medical treatments and increasing public awareness will propel the pharmaceutical device industry in the upcoming years.

The pervasiveness of cardiovascular problems, general health conditions, infections, and various other illnesses that comes with the increasing advancement of medical procedures and treatments and raising widespread attention will propel the pharmaceutical gadget market in the future years.

Several other diseases call for constant medical attention. Chronic diseases like diabetes, osteoporosis, arthritis, heart disease, hypertension, and dementia are typical of all the senior generation, and they also call for constant medical attention. Based on the American Geriatrics Society, approximately 30 percent of the 65 plus patient population in the US needs this number. Geriatrician care increases as nearly one-fifth of the US public will be more than 65 years old by 2030. This can have a good impact on the worldwide health-related polymers industry in the forecast period.

## Factor 5: Low Cost, Biocompatibility, and Longevity Polymers

Medical polymers are used for different types of medical devices. Medical polymers include biodegradable polymers, flexible and rigid PVC, nylon, polyurethane, and Teflon products

Medical polymers for different medical devices: are found for dressings, implants, implantable defibrillators, blood filters, automated analyzers, diagnostic and imaging devices, catheters, tubes, and surgical gloves. With a low cost, less weight, and biocompatibility, medical polymers are considered suitable for medical applications.[4]

A complementary factor is the boosting uses of polymers. Boosting polymers' applications, including polyether ether ketone (PEEK), polysulfone, polyphenylsulfone, and polyetherimide in pharmaceutical products, improves the worldwide health-related polymers industry through the entire forecast period.

Polyether-ether-ketone (PEEK), a high-performing biocompatible material, has made a grand entry in many medical applications. Evonik recently publicized that its Vestakeep-branded PEEK polymer is present in more than 80 medical equipment transparent by the FDA.

According to Grand View Reports, polypropylene emerges as the fastest-growing plastic for medical packaging, which forecasts a 9.2 percent CAGR for the material between 2017 and 2025.[5] The manufacture of the best quality plastic composites for specific applications to achieve a high product differentiation degree is growing.

## Factor 6: Applications in Diagnostic Systems

Medical polymers being biocompatible, have extensive medical devices, implants, disposable gloves, and tools. The cumulative shift toward biodegradable polymer products has directed to widespread medical polymer usage in various applications.

The medical polymer has a vast application in the diagnostic system, biodegradable hospital accessories, and implants market. The cumulative shift toward eco-friendly polymer products has directed to widespread medical polymer usage in various applications. Moreover, the rising demand for medical polymers can increase the demand for medical equipment manufacturers and the healthcare service provider industry, which causes the expansion of these industries. Indeed, a physician or a medical practitioner never wishes a call for multiple therapeutic interventions to remove an implant. This is the benefit of biodegradable hospital accessories.

Nevertheless, an implant ready from the eco-friendly polymer is built to degrade at a rate that gradually transports ton on the healing bone. An additional fascinating use for which eco-friendly polymers provide tremendous opportunities can be as the grounds for drug delivery either.

## Strategic Review of the Potential of Medical Plastics Market

The section focuses on-demand on assessing the potential of the medical plastic market mainly through the lens of investors, existing players, and new market entries. Our objective is to evaluate the six dimensions of the market dynamic. Moreover, our assessment based on scores of the index of the market potential (IMP Index) for Medical Plastic comprises six factors (see Figure 4.1):

1. Market structure
2. Technical potential
3. Product potential
4. Distribution potential
5. Geographic potential
6. Potential for developing strategic competencies.

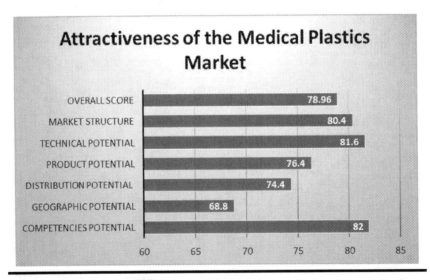

**Figure 4.1    Scores of the index of the market potential for medical plastic.**

Overall, the market obtains a score of 78.96. This is very good and could be assessed positively as a market with potential growth until 2025.

# Potential of the Market Structure

In total, the market structure is one of the positive aspects of the medical plastics market, with 80.4 percent. A first positive observation concerns the market structure for medical plastics. This market has a multitude of small niches that facilitate strategic entry into the medical plastic market. These niches provide good net cash flows once the company has established a position with a market share in its market.

## *Size of the Market*

The market has an exciting dimension and volume of activity that encourages investment. This market also has attractive profit margins that are relatively protected by the specialized nature of the goods sold. Margins are better in medical devices but less appealing in disposable products.

## *Norms and Standards*

In general, the norms and standards of the medical plastic market play an important role. A change in this market's rules and standards could lead to agitation among players not following the market's standards. However, these norms and standards are established companies.

In the medical plastics market, technical norms and standards are specialized and could be complicated. However, depending on the nature of the market segments, it varies considerably. The demand for disposable products here has much less developed technical standards than the market for medical devices for which reliability requirements are essential.

In general, the more sophisticated and complex the norms and standards, the better the margins.

## Market Domination by Large Competitors

The medical plastics market has several significant players that wield dominance. Several major players have developed complete product lines for the most profitable segments. However, several small niche markets in specialized sections allow companies to establish a competitive position.

The significant growth of these niches is attracting the entry of prominent players. When these niches keep growing, it could represent a problem. When a slot is reaching sufficient market size, it attracts significant players looking for profitable segments.

## Market Growth and Windows of Opportunity

Among the most decisive factors of this market is the growth rate, which is better than the plastics market, such as packaging. Growth rates offer windows of opportunities. However, we can estimate that this growth continues over the next 48 months, after which demand for medical plastics should experience a natural slowdown of its development.

## Buyer Price Sensitivity

Another advantage of the medical plastics market is that buyers are relatively insensitive to price than other markets served by the plastic industry.

As mentioned earlier, this price sensitivity decreases when the products' technical complexity increases, as is the case with medical devices.

# Potential for Technical Advancements

The technical potential is a suitable dimension. The professional potential faces the possibility of introducing products or services whose technicality increases the products and services' value and price. This dimension receives a very positive score of 80.4 percent, explained by the following factors.

## *Product Technical Development*

In general, medical plastics offer an excellent opportunity for technical product development. We note that the chance to develop specialized products adequately is unique. In most of the products, there are possibilities for product developments.

However, R&D is most important for the plastics market. Technical product development requires significant research and development continuously. Medical plastics require a significant technical product update of product lines. Innovative companies in the pharmaceutical market can renew nearly half of the products and services every five years.

## *Cost of R&D*

R&D costs of the medical plastics market are reasonable compared to that of technology in the aeronautics or software sectors.

However, research and development costs represent high sunk costs that significantly increase business risk. They can also represent a barrier to entry for a smaller company wishing to enter a market.

## Technical Development of Product Functionalities

One of the exciting features of the medical plastics market is that the technological development of products and new features are relatively easy to master. It is possible to take effect with a new feature, which would have a function to increase its value.

## Technical Development and Product Differentiation

The technical development allows us to have unique and easy to differentiate products. Several companies have distinguished themselves by new features. Research and development are critical to facilitate the technical differentiation of products. It could also allow a strategic entry into a new segment or geographic market.

However, when the technical development is not sufficiently sophisticated or does not involve several components, it could easily be copied.

# Potential for Product Design and Development

This market has excellent potential for product development with a rating of 76.4 percent.

## Product Range Development

One of the exciting factors of the medical plastics market is the possibility of developing a product range of 5 to 7 products sold under the same brand. A product range of 5 to 7 products attracts the interest of the buyers. In some markets, such as disposables, there is a proliferation of disposable products.

## Low Costs of Brand Extension

In the medical plastic industry, extending a brand with additional products offers an exciting opportunity. New products or services products could complement the existing current range of products and services. For example, several occasions are found in facilities with intelligent technologies and intelligent devices.

## Product Scope Economies

In the medical plastics market, a product range significantly decreases the cost of designing, selling, or distributing a product. The sharing of expenses is significant and offers economies of product scope.

The product range plays an essential role in decision-makers in buyers. When buyers have a variety of choices, they buy more. For example, the introduction of new products facilitates buyers if new products are introduced annually. These entries imply that it is often impossible to enter the market by selling a single product since the cost of sale and distribution is too high. It is then necessary to look for the distributor interested in distributing a unique product rather than a part of the product range.

## Value-Added from a Technical Point of View

In the medical plastic market, products add value from a technical point of view. Unlike other plastic markets, the medical plastics market makes it relatively easy to increase the number of products and buyers' prices.

## Switching Costs

Switching costs are costs that must be borne by the purchaser when changing product suppliers. The products offer possibilities to build loyalty with buyers.

The market for medical plastics may allow transfer costs to be made in specific niche markets. In general, in the medicinal product market, distribution involves high switching costs related to inventory management. It could also be explained by the buyer's risk aversion in healthcare.

Many service points and the complexity of the product lines make it often difficult for a buyer to change suppliers once established.

### Risk-Averse Profile of Buyers

This profile contributes to the establishment of stable cash flows. However, the risk-averse attitude of buyers might seriously complicate the entry into the market. For instance, hospital market purchasers are known to have an extreme risk aversion and block many innovative products' access. Purchases a problem in most hospitals because buyers may only accept a product that has received medical approval with detailed specifications. Most healthcare buyers purchase only based on costs for a set of given technical specifications. Purchasers often make it difficult to enter the market without a change in specifications by users or decision-makers.

## Potential for Distribution

The score of 74.4 percent is good at this dimension. The distribution potential refers to an opportunity to sell and distribute the products quickly. It also relates to pricing strategies for the different segments served. A distribution potential could be significant when the exact product could be sold with different pricing in various distribution channels.

Medical plastics products are becoming products accompanied by services. Thus, information reports and technical information, and professional training, are becoming an essential feature of the distribution.

## Regulation and Purchasing Policies

Another important factor relating to distribution is the regulation and purchasing policies. Products need to be facilitated to provide facilities that could be sold. Regulations are marking it challenging to enter several markets. In several cases, government contracts' geographical origin or requirements mean restrictions on the original products' limitation and copying.

One of the significant barriers is related to technical assistance. The product requires no more technical assistance than our current products. In many cases where medical plastics need substantial technical support, this reduces to some extent the ability to reach specific markets and expand globally.

## Technical Assistance

Technical assistance is an essential aspect of distributing products in the medical plastic market with two effects. The first positive effect is that it allows entry into geographical markets, representing the local market.

However, it represents an essential barrier since the coordination of 80 regional markets with technical assistance 24/7 often becomes the prerogative of multinational companies that have made companies' chairmanship in several geographic markets.

## Management of Complex Sales

In healthcare, the medical plastic market represents a complex sale. Complex sales also are known as Enterprise sales. It can refer to a trading method sometimes used by organizations when procuring large contracts for goods and services. The customer takes control of the selling process by issuing an RFP and requiring a proposal response from previously identified or interested suppliers.

Complex sales involve long sales cycles with multiple decision-makers. Moreover, various stakeholders and stakeholder groups contribute to every complicated purchase.

In the field of medical plastics, buying decisions can be complicated since it brings together several players. We find the prescriber who is often the doctor or nurse or a decision-maker who is the institutional head. The user is often the patient or the nurse. And in some cases, we find the normalizers who set technical standards. Finally, we see the buyers, either what purchases the buyers of all.

## Buyer Intentions

A final factor is related to buyers' buying intentions. In the medical plastic market, the purposes of buyers are good. Since plastics offer significant opportunities to reduce pharmaceutical product costs, the buyers are open to new product development. They also facilitate product miniaturization and replace other materials such as metal.

However, recycling has become an emerging purchasing criterion for buyers.

# Geographic Potential

This dimension refers to the potential for export outside its geographic market. For instance, when the geographic markets are homogeneous, it may or may not facilitate geographic expansion.

In the case of medical plastic, the score is good but has some strategic considerations.

## Economies of Geographic Scope

The scope of geographically significant economies occurs when there are geographic markets with a similar or related product. For example, this is currently the case in the medical plastics market. In medical plastics, regulations are increasing the cost of exporting.

In the medical plastics market, the markets are structured according to the major regional markets: The North American market, the European market, and the Chinese market. The three markets tend to have different regulatory frameworks. They also tend to adopt technological standards and standards that are different and not necessarily compatible. These different norms and standards increase complexity and business risk.

This situation is expected to change over the next five years as the harmonization of regulations between different countries and even different health systems facilitates the homogenization of the characteristics of geographic markets

## Regulatory Barriers to Block Entry

Another factor playing a role is the propensity of geographic markets to use regulatory barriers to block new players' entry. In the medical plastics market, since this market serves hospitals and local needs, buyers tend to introduce new regulations to make it more challenging to enter a local market, such as hospitals in each region.

However, in general, products are becoming more and more harmonized in terms of standards and manufacturing, facilitating geographical expansion. In that sense, it represents an opportunity.

## Harmonization of Regulatory Frameworks

However, in medical plastics, the harmonization of regulatory frameworks represents a longer-term risk for companies serving only one regional market. We need only think that harmonization of regulations facilitated the entry of Mexican products into the American market.

## A Critical Mass of Buyers Close to the Head Office

The geographical proximity to head offices and decision-makers is another crucial factor. For many companies in medical plastics, large equipment manufacturers are often located in large capitals. The geographic proximity of a company in medical plastics with a multinational has considerably facilitated its development.

However, in the plastic industry, several companies have traditionally been in the regions to reduce their operating costs. The location does facilitate building proximity with the headquarters of the major contractors.

# Potential for Developing Strategic Competencies

The scope of competence refers to the competencies that the enterprise must possess to compete in its market. So, in some markets, when the company must buy a supplier or a distributor, this increases its complexity. It also relates to the extension of competencies developed in the medical plastic market to serve other needs such as construction, mobility, electronics, and packaging.

## Value Creation for the Competencies of a Company

There is a broad range of skills since the knowledge and learning curve developed in the medical products market. It has excellent value for other promising needs with higher technological—technical intensity. New plastics generate for the medical market could be sold elsewhere. Companies active in the medical plastic market significantly increases the value of the or core skills.

## Economies of Scope Competencies

In the medical plastics market, the cost of sharing for tangible and intangible assets is essential. A company might share its cost of R&D for several markets. It might also use the same brand in several markets. For instance, when a company has developed a recipe, it can easily use the same method to serve other markets to offer additional products. It could also purchase expensive equipment and share it among different markets.

## Availability of Competent Suppliers

One of the potentials of a market is the availability of competent suppliers allowing the supply of added value and facilitating product development. There is enough volume of suppliers in the medical plastics market to facilitate strategic entry into this market.

## Risk of Vertical Integration from Suppliers

In the medical plastics market, the risk of vertical integration of suppliers is significant. The risk of copying and imitation by suppliers and therefore considerable. Suppliers have also been practicing a trading-up strategy. They enter off in a segment of cost-sensitive buyers to gradually increase their prices to serve all the market sections.

Therefore, it is essential that the sourcing covers only non-strategic aspects of a product or a plastic formula.

## Risk of Vertical Integration from Distributors

Another significant strategic threat in the medical plastics market is the vertical risk integration of distributors. In medical plastics, where volumes and ranges are high, distributors play a leading role and can make products outside China or copy and distribute them.

This threat is significant when the distributor occupies a considerable market share among buyers and is looking for a range of growth products. Vertical integration is found in disposable products that require little technical assistance.

## Transaction Costs and Legal Costs

There are significant risks and transaction and legal costs associated with the sale of medical plastics. While the medical plastics market offers exciting growth opportunities, it is also characterized by transaction costs and legal costs, such as lawsuits and contract breakdowns that are important. We are thinking of legal proceedings for defects in plastic products. But we also believe in contract breakdowns for changes in standards on buyers or manufacturers of products.

In many cases, the medical plastics market has transaction costs in terms of the quality and characteristics of the products and specifications requested by buyers.

# Notes

1. www.businesswire.com/news/home/20170127005227/en/ Biocompatibility-Versatility-Medical-Polymer-Implants-Driving-Global.
2. www.plasticstoday.com/medical/medical-plastics-market-hit-336-billion-2025-says-report/162414602557003.
3. Ibid.
4. https://www.gminsights.com/industry-analysis/ medical-polymers-market?gclid=CjwKCAjwq9m LBhB2EiwAuYdMtcX28b3fdzWWpLS4AsXWeM 3QP-c40caG2KMW_apu_BTuwXnJAp_KPBoCd-4QAvD_BwE
5. Op. Cit. www.plasticstoday.com

# Chapter 5

## Niches in the Medical Plastics Market

The medical plastics market offers several promising niches for new product development and applications. We review the following niches:

1. The antimicrobial market
2. Medical polymers
3. Synthetic polymers
4. Biodegradable synthetic polymers
5. Liquid silicone rubber
6. Bio-based and engineered biodegradable polymers for packaging
7. Bioresorbable materials
8. Disposable products
9. Single-use specialized gloves

## Niches of the Antimicrobial Market

The medical and healthcare program has dominated the antimicrobial plastics market. The increasing awareness explains

DOI: 10.4324/9781003212898-5

this regarding the usage of antimicrobial plastics. Increasing income levels of customers and increased spending on health and enhancing lifestyles in the area also meet the need for healthcare and healthcare programs.

The market for antimicrobial plastics is expanding geographically. Both North America and Europe are experiencing remarkable growth.

The Asian market, particularly China and India, is a new strategic location with untapped potential. Most Asian countries have thick population density and low income resulting from poor hygiene conditions. These markets are an opportunity for antimicrobial products.

To reduce costs, some companies adopt strategies resulting in the removal of antimicrobial protection. This method is affecting the dynamics of the plastic market by going against positive innovations. Surviving the competition without fighting for a price is essential to identify and invest in low-price applications such as heating, cooling, or ventilation.

Moreover, it is crucial to target a geographic market with less concern for prices initially in these emerging regions (Asia, Latin America, and Africa).

## Growth of the Antimicrobial Market

The antimicrobial plastics industry grew from USD29.6 billion in 2018 to USD43.1 billion in 2023, at a CAGR of 7.8 percent. The marketplace is primarily driven by the increasing need for antimicrobial plastics from uses, including packaging, automotive, consumer products, healthcare, building, &amp construction.

The growing need for antimicrobial plastics in upcoming apps has produced numerous opportunities for the makers. APAC is the primary sector for antimicrobial plastics internationally, followed by North America and Europe. Among the main drivers of the industry is the developing recognition of antimicrobial plastics in these areas. The American market of antimicrobial plastics is growing mainly in the health and medical market of packaging. There is a significant increase in the demand for antimicrobial products in the Healthcare sector and medical. This is one of the principal motives for the growth of this market.

We can note that the medical, health sector, and packaging, are by far the most sectors with high potential, respectively 44 percent and 24 percent of the antimicrobial plastics market. For example, these two sectors grew respectively 44 percent and 24 percent, to 46 percent and 27 percent between 2010 and 2014.

## Demand for Antimicrobial Products

The US market for antimicrobial plastics is mainly used in the healthcare, medical and packaging markets. There is a noteworthy increase in the call for antimicrobial products in the health and pharmaceutical sectors. This is the sole reason for the global growth of this market.

It should be noted that the medical, healthcare, and packaging sectors are by far the most requested sectors, with 44 percent and 24 percent of the market for antimicrobial plastics, respectively.

## Benefits of Antimicrobial Products

### Active 24/7

Antimicrobial protection is a permanent, inexpensive solution that remains active for your plastic product's expected lifetime.

### Redefines Clean

Antimicrobial plastic additives produce more durable and inherently cleaner plastic products. These unique features make antimicrobial plastics faultless for hygiene-critical, high-traffic environments such as hospitals, food processing facilities, and schools.

## Effective against Harmful Bacteria

Antimicrobial plastic additives lessen the occurrence of illness-causing bacteria on plastics. Tested strains include *E. coli*, *Campylobacter,* and antibiotic-resistant MRSA.

## Breaks the Mold

Antimicrobial plastic additives support your plastic product to fight the growth of unsightly mildew and mold.

## Stops the Stink

Antimicrobial conserves the aesthetics of plastic products purchased by the customer by minimizing odor and stain-causing bacteria.

## Increases Product Longevity

Microban's capacity to prevent the progress of degrading bacteria, mildew, and mold, means antimicrobial plastic products bought with your help from an increased life expectancy.

## Safe to Use

Antimicrobial plastic additives have experienced extensive independent laboratory testing and have a long history of safe use. The biocidal active components of Antimicrobial plastic additives are reported with the EU Biocidal Products Regulation (BPR) and recorded with the US Environmental Protection Agency (EPA).

## Food Contact Approved

Certain antimicrobial plastic technologies are food contact approved, listed on EFSA (European Food Safety Authority), and registered with the EPA.

## Growth Factors of the Antimicrobial Market

Epidemics such as COVID-19 in hospitals facilitate the growth of antimicrobial plastics. The growing number of people caught in an infection in the hospital enhances the value of antimicrobial products. This market is currently under development in the pharmaceutical and medical devices sectors. A variety of applications of these products are also growing in the health sector.

Unlike the health sector, with the COVID-19 pandemic, the industrial sector is still in its infancy for antimicrobial products. Although less regulated, the agri-food packaging sector requires the use of this type of product. Another opportunity, especially in North America, due to high demand, antimicrobial products are becoming increasingly powerful marketing tools in the sportswear industry.

# Niches of Medical Polymers

## Medical Polymers: An Essential Element of Medical Devices

Medical polymers have become an essential element of medical devices, allowing the emergence of the new generation of medical technology. They became an unavoidable component of medical devices, allowing the rise of the new generation of medical technologies.

Thanks to its lightness, low price, ease of use, flexibility, non-magnetization, and biocompatibility, the medical polymer has become an essential component of medical devices, allowing the appearance of the new generation of medical technology.

Global demand for medical polymers is estimated at 7 million tonnes for 2020.

## Replacement Materials

The replacement of materials is exponentially improving the polymer's mechanical and physical properties—plastic substitutes many products in the design of medical devices.

More than ever, plastic can compete with metal, and the convergence toward this material is already underway.

Many medical plastics are comparable to or even better than traditional materials when it comes to resistance, and they are lightweight, cheaper, more flexible, and easier to use.

## Medical Polymers' New Generation

Cost control becomes necessary for the medical device industry, and manufacturers turn to the supplier to reduce their costs (including polymer suppliers).

Suppliers help by innovating less expensive products and techniques while improving performance.

Medical device companies are interested in that their success is becoming recognized, generating numerous questions and surveys about them, mainly environmental. This ambient pressure forces some decisions that have not been made beforehand. The example of Bisphenol A, one of the most widely used products, has been challenged several times for environmental reasons before demonstrating its negative impact on the environment.

# Niches of Synthetic Polymers

Several biological, hybrid and synthetic polymers used for medical applications have more benefits being tunable in bodily, chemical, and natural qualities in a broad range to complement programs' demands.

This evaluation provides a short introduction about polymers' launch and innovations in medicine, dealing with initially functional polymers, consequently polymers with degradability as a very first biological feature, accompanied by many other practices and responsive polymers. It's shown up in which biomedical polymers comprise not just bulk substances but also coatings and pharmaceutical nano-carriers for medications. There is, consequently, an overview of the most often used polymer courses.

The assessment's primary body is structured based on the health applications, the applications' crucial demands, and the currently used polymer treatments.

# Niches of Synthetic Biodegradable Polymers

The medical plastics market offers many opportunities for synthetic biodegradable polymer plastics. They represent 50 percent of medical devices made of polymer. The polymer plays a vital role in the reduction of catheter infections and the manufacture of surgical instruments.

The technological innovation of advanced materials, such as nanoparticles, can transport drugs to damaged cells. The German medical plastics industry is investing heavily in the medical plastics market segment, particularly the nanoparticle market. Biomaterials also help in replacing damaged tissue and enhancing body functions.

According to *Plastic News*, biomaterials also help in replacing damaged tissue and enhancing body functions. Biomaterials are utilized for medical and aesthetic conditions. Because of pathological circumstances, injured, very soft, and tight fabrics are replaced with biomaterials to boost an individual's life expectancy.

All new biomaterials call for proof that they're safe and effective before they could be approved for promotion. In the United States, the approval procedure follows stringent regulations and guidelines set away by the United States agency on the Food and Drug Administration (FDA).

*Plastic News* further reports that biomaterials are likely to be approved as medical devices based on a 510-K or maybe premarket approval paths. Synthetic biodegradable polymers represent a promising niche in the medical plastics market for several reasons.

## Materials Made from Glycolic Acid

The survey showed that the ensuing polymers are extremely unstable for long-range industrial uses. The material made from glycolic acid and $\alpha$-hydroxy acids had to stop further development.

Nevertheless, this absolute instability—triggering biodegradation—has shown to be essential in healthcare uses during the last three years. Polymers ready from lactic acid and glycolic acid have noticed a wide range of healthcare industry applications, starting with the eco-friendly sutures initially approved in the 1960s.

Since that time, several items based on glycolic and lactic acid—and also on other materials, which include dioxanone), poly(trimethylene carbonate) copolymers, and also poly ($\epsilon$-caprolactone) homopolymers as well as copolymers—are recognized to be used as medical products. Along with these approved products, a good deal of research remains on poly-anhydrides, polyphosphates, polyorthoesters, along with any other eco-friendly polymers.

## Biodegradation Might Provide Various Other Benefits

The question is why healthcare practitioners would think about degrading material. There might be a range of motives, but the dullest starts with the physician's simple wish to have a unit that could be utilized as an implant and won't call for a second medical intervention for removal.

Apart from removing the demand for a second surgery, bio-degradation might provide various other benefits. For instance, a fractured bone that has long been fixated using a strict, nonbio-degradable stainless implant possesses an inclination for refrac-ture upon removing the implant. As the rigid stainless steel bears the strain, the bone hasn't been equipped to take an adequate ton throughout the recovery operation. Nevertheless, an implant ready from the eco-friendly polymer is built to degrade at a rate that gradually transports ton the healing bone. An additional fascinating use for which eco-friendly polymers provide tremen-dous opportunities can be as the grounds for drug delivery.

## Medical Grade Biodegradable Polymers[1]

This section examines *Medical Grade Biodegradable Polymers: A Perspective from Gram-Positive Bacteria* (2018). Globally, the increased need for fossil fuels for industrial plastics, scarcity of space for dumping, and constant environmental concerns for nonbiodegradable chemical-based plastics have promoted research toward sustainable development. The research on this product focused on eco-friendly, cost-effective, and biode-gradable polymers. Polyhydroxyalkanoates (PHA) have drawn much consideration as the suitable aspirant in this context.

Polyhydroxyalkanoates are both biocompatible and biodegradable polyesters, which thoroughly look like traditional plastics.

PHA technology and its copolymer production, though it is on a manufacturing scale, distribution and usage in varied manufacturing sectors are still limited due to the relatively high production cost. A high price is incurred due to the use of expensive, chemically synthesized carbon sources (~40 percent of the overall cost), making it hard to compete with petroleum-based polymers.

In this respect, labors are necessary to reduce cost and make it an environmentally benevolent procedure by the advancement of better bacterial straining, an active fermentation, and retrieval approach, use of small value, renewable resources (as carbon source) such as industrial waste, oil, glycerol, whey, cheese, molasses, starch, cane, wastewater, and fats. In the previous few years, renewable resources have attracted much curiosity in producing value-added products.

The current developments in biodegradable polymers in terms of their production process are going through the biotechnological route mainly by gram-positive bacteria using renewable resources and widely studied PHA applications (i.e., poly-3-hydroxybutyrate in different industrial sectors with an emphasis on the biomedical industry).

## Niches of Liquid Silicone Rubber

Silicone has made tremendous growth and opened up opportunities in the medical-related field. New health devices are emerging due to the biocompatibility of liquid silicone rubber (LSR). It's light on the epidermis, quickly removable, and lends itself to regulatory standards due to its high purity.

LSR is advancing in the industry of wearable device business. It ranges from patches to observe vitals and perhaps evolve to various other kinds of pieces employed for drug shipping.

All this medical equipment could today be realized due to electronic systems and these measurements, Wolf said. You want a substance that offers an excellent coating and process-ability in exposure to the skin. Liquid silicone rubbers are approved for skin communication in this type, and we've alternatives to embed electronic gear into the material in a way.

Dr. Wolf at the Silicone Elastomers US Summit of 2018 summarized the 3 Ps of LSR (Liquid silicone rubber) with properties, process, and performance.[2] LSR properties include okay hardness, tensile strength, excellent compression set, resistance to ozone, and low moisture and ultraviolet light absorption, he stated.

One attraction spurring the migration to LSR molding continues to be the profit margins, which may be recognized by the generation of LSR regions for the healthcare industry. The result has been stressed for businesses to support bills in an already overly competitive market.

Could LSR replace actual products? LSR, by itself, can't replace the world. But LSR can contribute a great deal toward entirely new solutions and innovations regarding megatrends to help make the planet's future even more sustainable. Robert Pelletier, a pro on dispensing of liquid silicone rubber said:

> current fashion in the healthcare industry include utilizing LSR in the generation of medical equipment components that require higher precision like seals, electronic connectors, sealing membranes, multi-pin connectors, and infant goods where sleek surfaces are desired, like bottle nipples and a couple of medical applications. . . . It is common in the generation of substances which are implanted in the entire body, like covers for leads on a pacemaker.[3]

## Niches of Bio-Based and Engineered Polymers

The development of bio-based and engineered biodegradable polymers for the packaging of medical products and medical disposables flourish the packaging application of the global medical polymers market. Medical packaging also rises substantially, owing to the mandatory disposal norms. This segment witnesses a CAGR of more than 9 percent in the forecast span.

All new biomaterials call for proof that they are safe and effective and should be approved for promotion. In the United States, the approval procedure follows stringent regulations and guidelines set away by the United States Food & Drug Administration (FDA).

Biopolymers are an organic and natural strain of polymer that is produced effortlessly by living things. However, there are some diverse classifications of biopolymers. The transparent plastic injection molding business is beginning to develop much more renewable materials for mass production.

The bulk of biomaterials utilized in humans are artificial polymers, reducing the risk of disease transmission. Biomaterial minimizes debris development, and its biocompatible chemical composition stays away from adverse tissue reaction.

Biobased resources produce a great deal of interest, but after comprehensive functionality tests and cost impact analysis, there's a reluctance to pay a high quality for them. "Most bio plasticizers have yet to prove themselves completely agreeable with PVC with the shelf-life of the device," noted Galland

# Niches of Bioresorbable Materials

Bioabsorbable materials are polyester-based and facilitate minimally invasive procedures.

## *Polyester-Based Bioresorbable Polymers*

A majority of bioresorbable polymers have been polyester-based, with two of the most common polylactic acid (PLA) and polyglycolic acid (PGA). However, new material is beginning to emerge. For more than two decades, bioresorbable has been a part of the plastics landscape.

But their usage in health devices has burst over the past few years. These resources, which worsen over time and are safely absorbed and excreted by the body, continuously find new applications in medication, particularly in the areas of drug distribution (e.g., drug-eluting stents), fixation (screws), and bone augmentation and tissue regeneration and replacement (scaffolds).

## Bioabsorbable Materials

According to *Plastic News*, bioabsorbable materials could help in facilitating minimally invasive procedures. Katen noted that "going back to the demographics, we see more lifestyle surgeries, such as joint replacements, and the bioabsorbable is being used in these areas." "The innovation in this place is truly science fiction stuff that is here now," he said.

The regulations in these areas are strict, as they should be. Being a manufacturer, supplier, and user, it is a moral duty of everyone to remember that the material in some form is going to be with a patient for the rest of life. In some cases, it may be a part of their body, too.

These materials can have a wide range of benefits, including orthopedic plates and pins. When made from a bioplastic, as an alternative to the old-style titanium, these devices gradually dissolve as they transmit load back to the curing bone. By abolishing follow-up surgery to eliminate the implant, these devices lessen healthcare costs and infection risk for patients.

## Niches of Disposable Products in Medical Plastics

There are various examples of specific applications for disposable products in the medical market, such as the following:

- Blood clot products such as a plastic catheter positioned in the artery developed specifically for medical use
- Prostheses: to correct malformations
- Artificial corneas: to treat eye injuries or chronic infections
- Hearing aids: to enable deaf and hard of hearing persons to regain a stable hearing
- Plastic drug capsules delivering the right dose at the right time

# Niches of Disposable Gloves

The single-use gloves market has reached $ 7.9 billion by 2020, with an annual growth of 6.2 percent.

According to Allied Market Research, the global disposable gloves market was valued at $6,146.2 million in 2016 and is likely to range $10,061.0 million by 2023, registering a CAGR 7.5 percent during the forecast period. The adoption of disposable gloves has increased over the years, owing to the rise in safety concerns and hygiene. COVID-19 increased this market growth significantly.

The disposable glove market reached USD7.9 billion by 2020, an annual growth of 6.2 percent.

However, Industry Insights, according to Grandview Research, the worldwide one-use gloves market scope was valued at USD8.19 billion in the year 2017. Rising demand for one-use gloves in healthcare and medical, automotive finishing, pharmaceutical, chemical, and oil and gas industries has been an essential factor driving the industry over the past few years.

## *Niches for Disposable Products Eco-Friendly Polymer*

According to *Plastic Research News*, disposable products could break down into three main eco-friendly polymer groups in the market: thermoplastic starch-based PHA, PLA, and polymers.

1. Thermoplastic starch-based polymers are derived from corn, tapioca, wheat, and potatoes.
2. PLA (polylactic acid) is polymerized from lactic acid derived from beets, corn, and other vegetables. Lactic acid is produced through the fermentation of sugar feedstocks.
3. PHA (polyhydroxyalkanoate) is generated in just a selected bacteria strain and saved as "fat." The fat is usually harvested, purified as well as utilized to produce a family of biopolymers.

## Notes

1. Swati Misra, A. K. Srivastava, Shailendra Raghuwanshi, Varsha Sharma, P. S. Bisen, 12—Medical grade biodegradable polymers: A perspective from gram-positive bacteria, Editor(s): Sabu Thomas, Preetha Balakrishnan, M.S. Sreekala, In *Woodhead Publishing Series in Biomaterials, and Fundamental Biomaterials: Polymers*, Woodhead Publishing, 2018, Pages 267–286, ISBN 9780081021941, https://doi.org/10.1016/B978-0-08-102194-1.00012-8.
2. https://www.dow.com/content/dam/dcc/documents/en-us/mark-prod-info/45/45-1590-01-lsr-solutions-market-trends.pdf?iframe=true.
3. https://www.plasticsnews.com/article/20160701/NEWS/160639958/closed-loop-important-in-lsr-molding.

*Chapter 6*

# Emergent Research for New Product Development

This section focuses on emergent trends and research topics to develop new products or modern applications.

## Patents on Medical Plastics

The medical plastics market has received many patents, around 15,000 over the last five years. This market represents a considerable amount and indicates the value of medical plastics technologies for companies and investors.

The evolution of patents for the medical plastics market has been relatively stable. The number of patents for 2019 was 28,658, representing a decrease of 12.5 percent compared to 2018.

The majority of patents were completed for the United States Patent & Trademark Office (Table 6.1).

DOI: 10.4324/9781003212898-6

**Table 6.1    Patents on Medical Plastics**

| ☑ | |
|---|---|
| *Evolution of Patent in Medical Plastics* | |
| 2019 | 28658 |
| 2018 | 32733 |
| 2017 | 37920 |
| 2016 | 36712 |
| 2016 | 36712 |
| *Distribution among Patents Offices* | |
| United States Patent & Trademark Office | 391,995 |
| Japan Patent Office | 129,73 |
| European Patent Office | 52,072 |
| World Intellectual Property Organization | 36,623 |
| United Kingdom Intellectual Property Office | 8617 |

# Emergent Research Topics for New Product Development and Applications

A survey of trending topics for research into medical plastics with SciVal Topic Prominence indicates that the following ten areas received the most exceptional attention. Their momentum rank topics with an indicator for the medical plastics market.

The top ten topics on the research on medical plastics for 2020 are listed in Table 6.2.

# The Top Researchers in the Medical Plastics Market Worldwide

The top researchers worldwide from the market of medical plastics ranked by the number of referred publications are as follows:

- Zhang, L. C. (20)
- Heller, L. (10)

- Liang, S. Y. (10)
- Šittner, P. (10)
- Lei, B. (9)
- Ning, J. (9)
- Tyc, O. (9)
- Chen, L. Y. (8)
- Chen, Y. (7)
- Finne-Wistrand, A. (7)

**Table 6.2    Topics on the Research on Medical Plastics for 2020**

| Serial Number | Name of the topics | Rank (Percent wise) |
|---|---|---|
| 1 | Melting, Additives, and Laser powder | 99.9% |
| 2 | Flexible electronics, Pressure Sensors, and Flexible strain | 99.9% |
| 3 | Scaffolds, Tissue engineering, and Scaffold fabrication | 99.4% |
| 4 | Elastomer, Liquid crystals, and Crystal elastomer | 98.7% |
| 5 | Brushes, Fouling, and Zwitterionic polymers | 98.5% |
| 6 | Polyurethanes, Elastomer, and Polyurethane elastomer | 96.5% |
| 7 | Laser heating. Sintering, and Laser sintered | 95.4% |
| 8 | Glycerol, Elastomer, and Sebacate PGS | 94.8% |
| 9 | Plasma polymerization, Plasmas, and Plasma polymers | 94.3% |
| 10 | Cotton fabrics, *Escherichia coli*, and Treated cotton | 93.6% |

# The Most Critical Research Disciplines in Medical Plastics

Research is coming from several disciplines. Every topic in Table 6.3 is ranked in order of its importance and the number of publications devoted to the subject.

## The Five Most Important Research Journals

The five most essential research journals for the medical plastics market are listed in Table 6.4.

# Review of Research Publications for Product Development and Applications

In the final section in this chapter, we review promising research that could lead to new product development and applications.

**Table 6.3   Critical Research Disciplines in Medical Plastics**

| Serial Number | Topic | Number of Publications |
|---|---|---|
| 1 | Material Science | 900 |
| 2 | Medicine | 867 |
| 3 | Engineering | 604 |
| 4 | Chemistry | 499 |
| 5 | Physics and Astronomy | 365 |
| 6 | Chemical Engineering | 304 |
| 7 | Biochemistry, Genetics and Molecular Biology | 289 |
| 8 | Environmental Science | 170 |
| 9 | Pharmacology, Toxicology, and Pharmaceutics | 95 |
| 10 | Energy | 93 |

**Table 6.4    Essential Research Journals for the Medical Plastics Market**

| Serial Number | Journal Title | Number of Published Articles |
|---|---|---|
| 1 | Plastic and Reconstructive Surgery | 2,244 |
| 2 | Journal of Plastic Reconstructive and Aesthetic Surgery | 773 |
| 3 | Aesthetic Surgery Journal | 588 |
| 4 | Annals of Plastic Surgery | 541 |
| 5 | Ophthalmic Plastic and Reconstructive Surgery | 488 |

## Improvements of Plastics for Hydrophilic Catheters in Medical Care[1]

Single-use health devices have been under closer scrutiny for many years, particularly the option of plastic materials. Several specifications, like healthcare security, therapy performance, productivity, and environmental performance, should be satisfied. The most often used components for hydrophilic urinary catheters are polyvinyl chloride (thermoplastic polyurethane and PVC) (TPU).

In this research, the environmental performance of these two materials was examined. If we consider the data acquired for that test, a new transparent plastic substance used in urinary catheters was created. The target for improving this brand-new material was designing a high-end material with superior, environmentally friendly performance. The newly established plastic material is a polyolefin-based elastomer. The environmentally friendly version of the newest content was evaluated as well as compared to modern plastic materials. The study concentrated exclusively on the option of plastic materials and their ecological and environmental performance.

■ The evaluation is conducted using a method perspective and a life cycle assessment (LCA) strategy. The purposeful device is set to the therapy of one affected person during one season. The results from the LCA designs have been given both in the terminology of immediate inventory data, like energy consumption and formed emissions, and in terms of the effect from four various impact assessment techniques

■ Analysis of the outcome is based on immediate inventory data. The standard inventory benefits are seen in energy resource use, $CO_2$, $SO_2$, and $NO_x$ emissions. These benefits show a general better green performance for the new polyolefin-based Elastomer than the current TPU and PVC plastic materials.

■ The weighting and normalization stages in the analysis have suggested the benefits of using energy sources and climate change as a signal for green performance even if other influence groups likewise could play a role. The polyolefin-based Elastomer displayed a far better green functionality in the eco-friendly impact assessment than the TPU material.

■ Compared to PVC transparent plastic material, the new polyolefin-based Elastomer displayed a nearly equivalent overall environmental performance. Transparent plastic keeps the ability to create high-quality products with better all-around ecological performance.

■ The various materials energy consumption may primarily clarify this. Researchers think using the transparent plastic formula as a base material in medical equipment production is the most performing formula. Thus, the fresh content has also proven to be a great eco alternative to PVC if a PVC-free material is requested. Transparent plastic is a boom in the medical industry.

## Perspectives on Alternatives to Phthalate Plasticized Poly(vinyl Chloride)[2]

This research examined the perspectives on alternatives to phthalate plasticized poly(vinyl Chloride) in medical device applications.

Poly(vinyl chloride) (PVC) is among the most crucial polymeric substances currently available and used to produce many clothes, ranging from toys and packaging to healthcare products. PVC is per se a rigid material though it's built softer by compounding with plasticizers, particularly phthalate esters such as di-(2-Ethylhexyl) phthalate (DEHP).

Inadaptable plasticizer PVC (P-PVC), phthalates usually are not chemically bound to PVC and introduced into the outside environment. Particularly, prolonged contact of P-PVC-based health products with tissues or body fluids has been proven to be reliable concerning severe health consequences.

Significant concerns about the safety of P-PVC in healthcare plastic products have been raised. Moreover, many phthalates and P-PVC options and the chemical/physical therapies of P-PVC to minimize DEHP migration have been recommended.

This evaluation outlined current scientific methods for stopping DEHP contamination of people by P-PVC medical products, highlighting the effect of the suggested substitute substances on human health and techniques for executing them.

## *Applied Plastics Boosts Capacity for Medical OEM*[3]

Several companies, such as Applied Plastics Co. Inc., are installing more custom-made processing equipment for coating large diameter wires for medical applications. The kit can handle tolerances of 0.001-in. The Norwood, MA, USA-based company provides fluoropolymer powder coating services for all kinds of parts demanding resistance to chemicals and corrosion. The coating is electrostatically applied in specific parts like valves, pumps, and mixers.

# Notes

1. 10.1016/J.JCLEPRO.2007.12.006.

2. Perspectives on alternatives to phthalate plasticized poly(vinyl chloride) in medical devices applications *Progress in Polymer Science* Volume 38, Issue 7, July 2013, Pages 1067–1088.
3. *Plastics Today News*, 28 Aug 2012, (Website: www.plasticstoday. com/) 2012.

*Chapter 7*

# An Assessment of the Competition in the Medical Plastics Industry

This chapter gives us insights into an assessment of the competition in the medical plastics industry. We review the structure of competition using Porter's model of five forces to identify opportunities and threats.

## Industry Definition

The most crucial thing to comprehend about the medical device industry is its product diversity. The US Food and Drug Administration (FDA) describes a medical unit in broad terms. This particular definition states, "instrument, apparatus, implement, machine, contrivance, implant, in vitro reagent, or maybe any other related or perhaps similar article, incorporating a portion, and accessory that is utilized in diagnosing, preventing, curing, and managing an ailment."

The industry of medical plastics has a strong presence of numerous companies catering to the neighborhood and

DOI: 10.4324/9781003212898-7

overseas marketplaces. These players are associated with the creation of differentiated products if they consider their performance characteristics. The presence of numerous businesses on the market results in a rise in the customers' purchasing power.

There are approximately 5,500 alone in the US engaged in the manufacturing of various medical devices. These companies are creating items that vary from human-made joints, bedpans to robotic therapeutic methods.

## Industry Overview

The industry of medical equipment is all about the manufacturing of electromedical and electrotherapeutic kits. It includes MRI equipment, therapeutic ultrasound equipment, pacemakers, hearing aids, electrocardiographs, and electromedical endoscopic equipment. Other products manufactured under these industrial units are irradiation apparatuses and tubes for medical diagnostic, medical therapeutic, industrial, research, scientific evaluation, and other applications.

Several of these medical device businesses are significant and highly lucrative. Nevertheless, more than 70 percent of them have fewer than 20 workers. Most of them continue to be in the development phase and have no consistent revenue.

The competitive characteristics for these companies vary significantly based on the product type they make. Secure medical devices, for instance, medical supplies, tend to compete mainly on price and usually have good profit margins. Medical devices that use advanced technology tend to have fewer competitors but require sunk costs in R&D for product development.

The FDA controls most medical products in the US. The company puts a medical unit in one of three classes. And the cases are as follows:

# Structure of Competition

The competition structure analysis in the medical plastics market has noted that the demand intensifies for 2000–2025 and requires a competitive positioning to maintain net cash flows.

The Industry Attractiveness Index (IA Index) was developed and used to measure and assess the industry's attractiveness. We use the structure of competition in the medical plastics industry as the primary source of information (Figure 7.1).

## *General Considerations*

An overall score of 75 percent.

The competitive index of the medical plastics industry receives a correct score of 75 percent. If market growth is attractive, the industry structure remains very competitive. Several factors are explaining the increase in the intensity of competition.

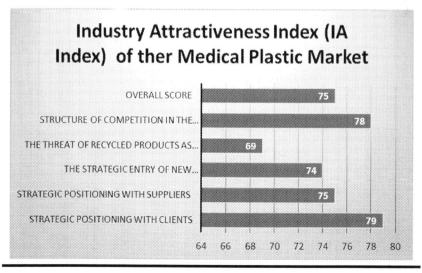

**Figure 7.1   Industry attractiveness index (IA Index) of the medical plastic market.**

## Concentration with Multinationals

Large multinationals control a significant concentration of the market, and the strength keeps increasing. Multinational players like Bayer's and DuPont are active in all profitable product ranges with a broad distribution in many geographic markets.

## SMEs Occupy the Largest Share of the Medical Plastics Market

On the other hand, many small and medium-sized enterprises often specialized in a single product or a narrow range of products. These market specialists are usually present in a single geographic market that competes with a limited range of products and often works with distributors to promote their products. Often, they have also awarded substantial contracts to suppliers. Despite the coated and specialized nature of their strategy, smaller businesses are more vulnerable to market fluctuations.

## Chinese Companies in Value-Added Segments

The third important factor is the rise in Chinese manufacturers' power, already very present in the plastic industry. However, after invading the niches of disposable products, they are now investing in medical devices by proposing complete solutions to customers. Japanese companies have a strategy in the medical plastics market as they do in other markets with a trading-up approach.

This strategy consists of offering products with attractive prices then gradually trade-up the low-cost segments by increasing costs to invade other more upscale sectors. Thus, Chinese companies' generic plan consists of learning the trade of medical plastics by being the supplier for critical components for a few years. 1) The companies obtained spare parts contracts from various western manufacturers. 2) They can assemble the separate agreements' different components to compete by presenting complete and integrated products.

# Strategic Positioning with Clients

The strategic positioning of clients and distributors receives a positive score of 79 percent. Plastic medical companies establish a competitive position based on product differentiation and technological advancement. The following factors explain this good score obtained for the situation regarding clients.

## *Surf on the Aging of the Population*

Technological advancement has increased healthcare spending, and the improving economy has stimulated demand for medical devices over the past five years. The aging US populace has contributed more to industry revenue, given the high incidence of health issues requiring medical devices among older adults.

## *High Prices Coming from Technological Development*

Technological advancement has increased healthcare spending, and the improving economy has stimulated demand for medical devices over the past five years.

## *The Two-Tiered Trading Power of Clients*

The trading power of customers is two-tiered. A significant opportunity to increase the value of medical plastics is the technical development of the products. As we intend to see in the following section, several elements, including aspects affecting the quality of the product, such as the quality of the plastic, the reliability of the equipment, and items relating to the biodegradability of the products, are essential factors that can increase power over buyers.

Multinationals' prerequisite offers a complete solution of integrated systems by controlling the suppliers and distributors in the support and service sectors. Considering smaller companies and their power to attract customers increase significantly, as greater availability of manufacturers is made possible by the Chinese investors' increased presence.

## Growth in Spending on Medical Devices

As per the US Survey, spending on therapeutic devices has been persistent over a span from 2005 to 2015. Over the previous decade, the consumer price index (or CPI) increased by 2.4 percent, and the medical care (or MC-CPI) consumer price index rose by 3.6 percent. However, therapeutic device prices have witnessed a usual yearly increase of only 0.7 percent. As validated by the National Health Expenditure (or NHE), an equal percentage of growth in medical devices' expenditure and the comparatively slow rate of rising prices highlight the highly viable nature of the health device manufacturing and considerable cost pressures.

## Higher Bargaining Power toward Clients with the Emergence of Platforms

There is an emergence of electronic platforms that are increasing the distribution and bargaining power over clients. Large multinationals are investing in an electronic platform to facilitate delivery and inventory control. Therefore, large multinationals invest heavily in distribution platforms to control the distribution. The power of media might become a significant issue over the next five years.

## Increased Pressure on Prices

Customers are putting tremendous pressure on prices for specific categories of plastic, including disposable products. Plastic processors serving the healthcare industry also see platforms expanding into inexpensive manufacturing areas to use low-cost labor. Frequently, these products are the ones that get exported to the US's country to be able to extend product lifecycles.

## The Power of Prescribers Shadows the Market

In the medical plastics market, prescribers, particularly in medical devices, disturb the smooth flow of market movement by exerting an influence that could facilitate product differentiation. The power of medical authorities, such as doctors, is a critical component of market leaders' strategy. This approach by companies is familiar because they are already active in the area of pharmaceuticals with physicians.

This strategy consists of obtaining referrals from physicians via prescriptions or specifications to create loyalty to the recognized product brands. It is strategic and multinational, but its cost is higher for smaller companies.

## Trust of OEMs and Design Engineers

The need for transparent plastic in health units is increasing day by day, with the need to help boost performance and lower costs. The viability of metal to plastic sells itself for both engineers and companies with minimum plastic skills finding the changing trend a challenge. For them, the complex world of polymer is not making any sense. The range of polymers offers you thousands of choices to select the best sheet for healthcare products.

Apart from this, deciding cost, the material's performance, and manufacturers' ability to produce the desired outcome are the main obstacles. While numerous diverse factors need careful attention, the main critical point is how the device is used.

For instance, health-related unit OEMs and design engineers could significantly narrow the polymer applicants' area by thoroughly defining end-user needs in the beginning and consulting their supplier at the start of the design operation. Proper guidance on material evaluation makes manufacturers and device designers concentrate on production rather than promoting a device. Matching performance needs with polymer abilities is the area of their expertise. Also, they may quickly help you in the proper path, which can narrow your choices.

## Regulations Are Standardizing Products

The biocompatibility testing methodologies and programs provided by the International Organization for Standardization are adopted in the medical and healthcare sector. Suppose one wishes to refer to other country-specific guidelines on biocompatibility testing outside of the US. The test results, like ISO-10993, are most suitable for applications in the United States. The selected testis-10993 program and biological endpoints are subject to several different factors, including the time and duration of contact with the device.

## The Emergence of Remote Health Control Monitoring

Continuous monitoring is a strong emergent trend in medical devices. There is a potential for real-time data shortly that could change the situation with clients.

## Strategic Positioning with Suppliers

The strategic positioning versus suppliers receives a positive score of 75 percent. Plastic medical companies can establish a competitive position with suppliers and sourcing. But the access to the advanced materials and the risk of vertical integration of suppliers represent a credible threat.

## Acquisition of Critical Suppliers

Companies have pursued to balance rising costs in manufacturing by outsourcing work and acquiring minor companies with pioneering technologies.

In the medical plastics market, manufacturers use subcontracting during production. For example, plastic injection and blending are outsourced activities that are on the rise. Manufacturers of medical devices are looking for specialized subcontractors and focusing on assembly. The selection of subcontractors is tight: high compliance requirements, regulatory understanding, and component reliability.

The determination of subcontractors relies on the following factors: the demonstrated ability to design medical devices, financial stability, the reputation of quality products on the market, cost containment, and the added value. The subcontractor could provide sterilization, assembly, and packaging.

As shown in Figure 7.2, Medical Plastics Devices and Medtech have performed very well over the past five years. According to SRR (Stout Risius Ross, a business magazine), their performance indexes have increased by 39.7 percent and 16.3 percent, respectively.

## Development of Advanced Materials

Resin is the material for which suppliers are under much higher pressure than before. The products are commonplace and are primarily subject to price competition.

It is only the development of advanced materials such as plastics of better quality or with new properties that can allow a company to lose its negotiating power from suppliers.

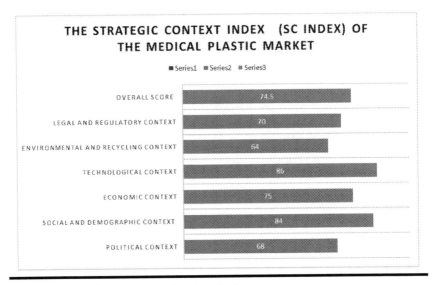

**Figure 7.2   Industry attractiveness index.**

## *Preemption Over Critical Suppliers*

However, most strategic suppliers in advanced materials are acquired by multinationals that control research and development.

Smaller and independent medical plastics companies are often subject to the vagaries and the technical requirements of the suppliers of materials and equipment. They usually do not have access to the latest innovations.

## The Strategic Entry of New Competitors

The strategic positioning of medical plastics providers versus suppliers receives a correct score of 74 percent. Plastic pharmaceutical companies can establish barriers at the entry to protect their market by investing in new product development. However, strategy entries are made possible by the proliferation of small niches in several geographic markets.

The market in medical plastics is structured with significant barriers for the most lucrative niche markets. Multinationals control not only the distribution but also the supply via the acquisition of suppliers. But they also actively erect entry barriers into the market of medical plastics.

## Reduced Barriers to Globalization

Reduced blockades to globalization have shifted overseas manufacturing presence. Overseas growth has comfortably outpaced domestic growth. This has tremendously changed the value of exports by taking it as low as $11.9 billion; the amount of imports has increased 4 percent annually to $17.3 billion.

### Strategic Entry and Mobility in the Market

Between 2015 to 2020, a brand-new product received an effective development method by leading companies like Celanese Corporation, Eastman Chemical Corporation, and Dow Chemical Corporation. Additionally, businesses like GW Plastics likewise resorted to capacity expansion to increase market shares and revenues.

### Reputation and Intangible Assets

The most critical barrier to entry is related to a company's reputation. Most purchasers want to do business with a large, established company free from the risk of lawsuits or manufacturing defects. Building a corporate reputation requires significant investment in advertising and promotion to medical buyers and prescribers.

### Investment in Research and Development

Research and development divestments via research laboratories are increasingly crucial in its prerogative multinationals to penetrate the medical plastics markets.

However, most independent market specialists are more interested in developing new products than their functions or processes. Buyers are susceptible to a company's ability to implement a new product development program.

## The Battle for Distribution

Distribution costs to enter the medical plastics market can be high. We think about technical assistance to clients with local distributors, promotional activities in tradeshows, and electronic platforms' development necessary to control medical plastics products' distribution.

## The Case of Strategic Entry with New Product Development

A feature and the development of new products mainly drive the medical plastics market. The good news is that a company can enter this market with a single product. A company's entry strategy must develop a new product whose functionalities better meet buyers' needs.

Recent plastic medical devices focused on products such as:

Custom Modeling: medical plastic devices generally start as custom injection molders for the medical devices and pharmaceutical industries. We have built a reputation for first-class molding and excellent customer satisfaction.

For example, MPD Inc. is a custom sealing company sealing equipment to make products from various plastic films such as PVC for the medical market. Current products include different medical bags, with and without ports and tubes, and covers for surgical devices, to name a few.

High-end medical and food-grade injection mold plastic manufacturing provide injection molding and product assembly in a purpose-built clean room with advanced robotics.

A strategic entry in the medical plastics market could also be achieved with innovative processes, as one executive mentions: "Using our in-house pre-production tooling, we work with you on New Product Development to achieve a higher market speed. If you plan to grow internationally through innovative plastic products that require absolute precision, then we are your total solution."[1]

## A Strategic Entry Facilitated by 3-D Printing in Some Segments

3-D printing, also known as the Additive manufacturing sector, has enjoyed sustained double-digit growth in recent years. It is estimated to be worth more than USD7.5 billion by 2020 (McKinsey & Company, 2013, Whalen & Akaka, 2015).

There are opportunities to adopt this technology in critical sectors such as automotive manufacturing, medical devices, aerospace, implants, power generation, and the creative industries (Green, 2015). Many companies across the US have already assessed the technology. Several of them have started using it on a minor scale.

Also, 3-D printing technologies, due to their digital nature (Pearce, 2015), could decrease energy, materials, and water by eliminating waste, together with all additional detrimental process enablers, thus having a positive effect on sustainability (Cozmei & Caloian, 2012).

The adoption of 3-D printing inspires alternate business models and supply-chain management approaches. 3-D printing aims at modifying the need for freeing up working capital within the supply chain, affluent tooling, and reducing business risk in new product development and innovation (Bessen et al., 2012).

There is a growing perception among innovation scholars and brand business experts that 3-D printing creates a new wave of adopting technology associated with the rise of various business prospects for both existing and tech entrepreneurs.

Additive manufacturing or 3-D printing is one of the most promising emerging technologies coming to the market with a potentially disruptive power. After around three decades in the making, 3-D has shifted from being an industrial rapid prototyping technique to an ordinary industrial process used by industry and consumers alike. Looking at the international landscape of innovation, technology, and entrepreneurship, developments around 3-D printing have grown thrust and momentum across all news channels. The plethora is raising high expectations regarding its potential in revenue generation.

According to a study conducted by Deloitte, the most significant change in this regard is a move away from plastic and toward metal printing. Plastic is so far suitable for prototypes and some final parts. The trillion-dollar metal-parts fabrication business is the more significant market for 3-D printers to report. Between 2017–2018, a 3-D printing manufacturing study showed that, although plastic was still the most common material, its share in 3-D printing fell from 88 percent to 65 percent in that single year alone, while the share of metal printing increased from 28 percent to 36 percent. At that rate, it seems possible that metal surpasses plastics and represents more than half of all 3-D printing by 2020 or 2021.

## The Threat of Recycled Products as Substitutes

The strategic positioning versus substitutes and replacement product receives only a score of 69 percent. Recycling of products has become a new preoccupation with buyers. The strategic positioning versus reserves introduces competition of recycled products that are complexifying the distribution process and putting pressure on the price.

While medical plastics have contributed to replacing a significant range of products in this sector, competition from substitutes and alternatives has declined.

## Recycling and Environmental Concerns

One of the essential factors regarding the risk of substitution relates to recycling and environmental concerns associated with medical plastics products.

In the next five years, the biodegradability of medical plastics products becomes much more critical than before. It could recover health and substitutes for the products that are present in the market.

Recycling in the hospital market has become a significant concern for buyers who want to find a solution to this problem.

## The Concept of the Sustainable Product Life Cycle

A final factor in the risk of plastic substitution is the concept of the sustainable product life cycle. It involves putting pressure on manufacturers to reuse and take back the plastics sold to offer new ones. The disposal of medical products is under further pressure. It could lead to the emergence of high-level substitutes that provide solutions to the removal of pharmaceutical products.

# Structure of Competition in the Medical Plastics Market

The rivalry among medical plastics companies receives a correct score of 78 percent. The industry's fragmented structure and the intense competition from a large number of companies explain this score. It is defined mainly by a. Consolidation in the industry might reduce the rivalry's intensity in the next five coming years.

Even with the consolidation in the multinationals' medical plastics market in recent years, medical plastics' demand remains fragmented. Technical innovation contributes significantly to maintaining the number of independent companies.

Market consolidation is substantial and decreases the number of medium-sized enterprises dominating a geographic market. Once a company in medical plastics controls a geographic market, it is often the subject of an international acquisition. This acquisition aims first to better control distribution on the geographical market. It also seeks to block the entry of local players.

SME's often have privileged access to public procurement and the medical community. They could offer products adapted to buyers' specifications in their territory and build proximity with buyers in this market.

## Consolidation with Mergers and Acquisitions

The market accelerates its consolidation with mergers and acquisitions. For this reason, margins are expected to increase slightly to 4.8 percent. Regardless of fear of changes to the 510(k) FDA approval procedure, growing supervisory costs, and reducing innovation in 2013, the industry saw active growth in the M&A field, with progress increasing over 50 percent in 2017.

The consolidation generally results in the growth of functional inefficiencies in an enterprise to obtain scale and access new products and technologies that may be disruptive for price building. Restructuring and streamlining the procedure and supply chain ability are essential for enterprises looking for inorganic expansion. Additionally, inventory streamlining and cost-efficient logistics operations improve the medical unit cost structure for a unit manufacturer.

## Mergers and Acquisitions Are Structuring the Medical Plastics Market

The market for medical plastics is gradually structured through mergers and acquisitions to acquire shares in this high-growth market.

Purchasers have been very active since 2012, with 74 percent of their purchases coming from injection molding and extraction companies.

Companies in the field of medical plastics are coveted companies in the market. Medical plastics users mainly focus on acquiring and merging into infrastructure, including sterilized parts and specialized capabilities, with the potential to become significant suppliers in the market.

## Competitive Market Share of Medical Polymers

Competition in the medical plastics market is structured with five strategic groups. The companies holding the largest market share in the Medical Device Manufacturing in the US industry include Medtronic PLC, General Electric Company, Abbott Laboratories, and Danaher Corporation.

## Revenue Volatility

Medical device companies are generally protected from significant revenue volatility. However, these products are also relatively expensive, making the Medical Device Manufacturing industry slightly more vulnerable to fluctuations in economic conditions.[2]

Average selling, administrative, and general (or maybe SG&A) costs incurred by medical device companies are around 36 percent of total revenues as per Advamed's 2015 report. Players that are big in the high and low-tech amount segment experience substantially higher SG& A bills than high tech niche players, which acquire higher development and research (or maybe R&D) costs.

## New Business Models to Lower Distribution Costs

Various models and strategies are now being used by players that are big to deliver enhancement in product sales operations in addition to a decrease in indirect expenses as part of SG& A's cost-containment measures.

For example, medical device companies such as Wright Medical (Cardinal Health and Wage; CAW) have multiple representatives and decided to sell fewer product sales models. These two actions have enabled substantial SGA expense minimization by slashing advertising as well as exercise costs.

## A Strong Differentiation of Large Players Based on R&D

Best health-related unit players invest somewhere between 6 percent and 12 percent of revenues to R& D investment. For smaller companies, technology and originality are differentiating elements. Consequently, R&D expenses remain important price pieces that operate the long-range productivity of companies.

For example, Medtronic (MDT) makes considerable R&D investments but watched a decline of 9.4 percent in 2013 to 8.7 percent in 2014. Nevertheless, for a niche firm as Illumina (ILMN), R&D spending rose from 22 percent to 24 percent from 2013 to 2014, respectively.

However, significant players make relatively smaller-sized investments in R&D in contrast with high-tech companies and concentrate on boosting productivity and margins via growing services and scale.

## A Market Based on Product Differentiation

Several factors have an impact on medical plastic products. These factors greatly influence the outcomes and their sales strategy in the various distribution channels. The competition in the market relies on product differentiation with factors such as the following:

■ Design differentiation
■ Multiple functionalities
■ Technical performance
■ Sustainable development
■ Security

## A Fragmented Market

A high level of competition is apt to strengthen customer purchasing power. Product quality and cost competitiveness are the main factors impacting the customer power decision.

Increased production volumes and the simplicity of accessibility of healthcare plastics operate the customer energy within the next couple of years.

## The Fierce Competition of Disposable Products

It is a market where price competition is fierce. It is becoming more and more controlled by Chinese companies with complete product catalogs and compete heavily on prices. Innovative products are quickly copied if the products in this category, offering little differentiation adds value. The sale of these products is under the control of professional buyers and supply systems whose purchasing criteria are standardized.

## Vertical Integration to Control Critical Suppliers

A remarkable phenomenon of medical plastics relates to the vertical integration of significant suppliers. One of the competitive advantages of multinationals in medical plastics is their control over the activities of suppliers. Its companies have acquired several technology suppliers to control the development of new advanced materials.

This acquisition also constitutes a barrier to entry and makes it more challenging to develop new products for independent companies vertically integrated.

Ever since the 80s, executives in medical plastic manufacturing corporations have faced a central strategic issue regarding the integration of suppliers. Finally, they seem to have found the right balance with a selective integration of suppliers and shared norms and standards of operations for engineering among suppliers.

In choosing to integrate backward due to apparent short-term rewards, managers usually restrict their ability to strike out in revolutionary directions in the future.

The industry is characterized by multiple vertical integrations in the medical plastics market through different value chain phases. For instance, HELM-AG is incorporated across all four steps in the value chain, from raw material production to the manufacturing and plastic production of end-use items used by the hospitals and healthcare institutions such as private clinics. Consider hot-metal making and steel manufacturing, two stages in the traditional steel industry chain. Vertical integration is a means of directing the various steps of an industry chain when joint trading is not advantageous.

## Vertical Integration to Control the Distribution

Another phenomenon is the vertical integration of distributors. In the medical plastics market, a company that not vertically integrated and, to some extent, thanks to its distributors. In many cases where the company has only one product or a small range of products, it must agree to pay the significant transaction costs in negotiating with distributors for its market. Moreover, several distributors have a propensity to make next to the products they distribute successfully.

Therefore, multinationals are acquiring distributors to control market access in a country. The acquisition of distributors also makes it possible to develop a social capital of proximity with the territory buyers. But the most significant thing is that the acquisition of a distributor makes it possible to control the prices and the efforts made to sell the company's products.

We found four reasons that were mentioned for the medical plastics market to integrate vertically:

- The marketplace is unreliable and risky, too—it "fails."
- Vendors in adjacent phases of the market chain have much more industry energy than businesses in the stage.
- Integration would develop or even exploit industry energy by elevating entry barriers or allowing cost discrimination across client segments.
- Companies should incorporate market development by integrating critical stages of design and production.

For example, PM Mold is a vertically integrated manufacturer that supports the entire plastic manufacturing process from product development to distribution. The result is a more efficient product development process with lower costs and more profits.

## Switching Cost Built with Medical Devices

Another strategic factor defining the rivalry is building switching costs. The transfer cost line refers to the costs a customer must pay to change the supplier. In the case of medical devices, the costs may be high.

Switching costs are particularly steep for medical devices. Many established companies no longer produce only equipment but also provide an information system.

Companies concentrate on strategic tie-ups with medical items and manufacturing companies' components, which results in an ensured need for plastics. Additionally, these companies can also be integrated into producing raw materials and medical-grade plastics, resulting in reduced raw material procurement and overhead costs.

## Business Systems to Better Control Costs

In terms of injection molding, the task economically turns out many regions, even those with complicated geometries. As an outcome, plastic has displaced metal in a broad range of uses in which the high cost of metal fabrication is cost-prohibitive.

Expense likewise is a critical development driver fueling the change to products that contain far more plastics as producers feel pressure to minimize instrumentation price. The cost control is causing a push toward higher volumes that favor plastic-made mass production strategies rather than the usual creation with metals.

## Increasing Needs to Manage the Costs of Medical Products

A significant pattern for plastics in healthcare continues with the increasing need to manage medical products' costs. There remains a growing strain on the market to keep costs in check.

Furthermore, cost control is an essential factor in the medical devices industry, so the manufacturers turn to the supplier to reduce their costs (including polymers).

Suppliers help by innovating products with less expensive techniques while improving performance.

# An Intensification of the Rivalry

Lean manufacturing is a concept used in creating lean strategies. The purpose is to build trust and keep the active manufacturing company attainable. The *Plastic News* report says that lean manufacturing minimizes production costs by reducing inefficiency, waste, and quality enhancement. Using and getting responses from people regarding a product line ensures the manufacturers make a product that satisfies actual users' needs. Viewing things from customers' perspectives is an essential concept in lean manufacturing.

Additionally, the buyer's feedback suggests that no material should be wasted on creating a solution that does not match the customers' requirements. The objectives and integrated method of lean manufacturing together increase efficiency on the manufacturing floor in several ways. Adaptable and embedded systems are essential to compete globally.

According to Jamie Flinchbaugh, a founder and a partner of the Novi, Michigan-based Lean Learning Center,

> manufacturer should search for adaptable devices which are typically customized to enhance the procedure, to save time, and minimize the errors. The mixture and co-existence of lean machine and manufacturing vision process integration reduce time and waste, increases productivity and production, enhances quality, and benefit organizations. Employees gain influence, responsibility, and expertise.[3]

## *Three Strategic Groups of Competitors*

Medical plastics have a market structure with the following groups:

## Large Chemical Companies

The first group consists of companies that are first and foremost chemical companies produced from plastic, such as DuPont and Celanese, Bayer-AG, Eastman Chemical, Dow Chemical, Evonik Industries, and Huntsman.

The chemicals companies are often only in markets and parts for which the margins are attractive. These companies are generally vertically integrated and have acquired suppliers and distributors to control market access and the supply of critical components.

## Large Pharmaceutical Companies

A second group is manufacturers from pharmaceutical sectors such as Johnson and Johnson. They are market generalists coming mainly from the pharmacy market. These companies are very familiar with medical specifications and have privileged access to doctors for referencing and equipment prescriptions. This service is essential as the market for home medical devices is growing significantly. This device is generally prescribed by doctors and reimbursed by insurance companies.

## Product Specialists

The third is only a group of product specialists, and there is a multitude of companies. Most often, product specialists serve only one category and one segment of the product. Therefore, a single product line is usually a unique product offered in a single geographic market, generally via a single distribution channel such as direct sales in hospitals. These businesses often survive through hospital purchasing policies that are beneficial to local businesses. They can offer local services, too.

Product specialists maintain close relationships with local hospitals and doctors. It is carried out mainly from the admiration of existing products that do not adequately research and develop. They are subject to the vagaries of developing new materials because it does not control the suppliers. They are also subject to distribution notions because they must transact via large distributors or even direct delivery on a smaller scale.

## Notes

1. https://www.medplas.com/developmentengineering/.
2. www.ibisworld.com/united-states/market-research-reports/ medical-device-manufacturing-industry/.
3. https://www.industryweek.com/operations/continuous-improvement/video/22012289/developing-people-with-a3-thinking#:~:text=Jamie%20Flinchbaugh%20is%20a%20founder,as%20Chrysler%20and%20DTE%20Energy.

## Chapter 8

# Factors Critical to Successful Competition in the Medical Plastics Market

## Introduction

The present medical plastics companies are under tremendous pressure to promote and deliver items faster than their competitors. This section helps in analyzing the essential factors to compete successfully in the medical plastics market. Here, we have provided the list of five identified factors:

1. Patient-centric design
2. Materials required for plastic medical devices
3. The critical role of technical specifications
4. The essential role of medical grade plastics
5. Continuous product development

DOI: 10.4324/9781003212898-8

# Key Factor of Success # 1: Patient-Centric Design

According to *Plastic News*, support for designing medical plastics devices centered on the patient's experience is becoming a more vital priority than ever. Resources for preparing with plastics are expanding within the pharmaceutical industry.

## *Toward More Ergonomic Products*

According to Mark Bonifacio, a veteran of the medical plastics industry and founder of Bonifacio Consulting Services, there is a focus and maybe even a return to patient-centric design. "This return to patient-centric design moves away from older products that are being re-made into more ergonomically and more accessible items for patients and care providers to handle," he said. "There is almost a consumer-type approach. There also is a move to lightweight and move from an engineered TPE to a commodity resin through a design change to lower the cost," he added.

## *Designing a Medical Product with Forte Plastics*

Bonifacio also noted that traditionally, processors have worked only with metals to adopt and generate expertise with plastic manufacturing methods. "With steadily increasing healthcare costs and advancement in technology, designers across the medical field are learning to intensify performance and cut costs through the utilization of specialty plastics," he explained.

According to *Plastic News*, Dr. Stephen Spielberg, president, and co-founder of Cambridge Polymer Group noted a severe concern about some plasticizers, specifically DEHP (a softener for polyvinyl chloride (PVC), a plastic polymer used in an extensive range of products). It has resulted in the development of alternative plasticizers, particularly in the area of pharmaceutical delivery containers. "With the development of new materials comes the need for new methods of testing them, particularly their long-term performance in vivo," Dr. Spielberg said. "We and others are working hard in this area. We are seeing more manufacturers of polymers offering their materials to sell for medical applications, and often we are providing biocompatibility data to support these applications," he explained.

## Introducing New Ways to Use Permanent Implants

A new approach to use permanent implants is needed from a decade ago when some companies, fearful of litigation, refused to sell resins for medical applications. For processors, the mechanical properties of materials affect how they are in device design. It is in terms of creep under load, fatigue performance, wear behavior, and other trends.

Another drift is how materials used in permanent implants react to the in vivo environment. A common goal with most of the implants has minimum material in an implant. It helps in sparing without compromising the smooth functioning of the implant. Strong, robust, and more resilient materials assist in serving that goal.

# Key Factor of Success # 2: Material Requirements for Plastic Medical Devices

Materials requirements play a crucial role in plastic medical devices.

## Reliable Performance Needs by Production, End-Use, Shipping, Packaging, and Disposal

Numerous instruments, and systems, are sterilized before delivering for the final usage. These devices contact different chemical substances, organs, skin, bodily fluids, solvents, and tissues during production and end consumption. The materials used in such products should not be reluctant to the sterilization techniques, chemicals, and liquids. It shall work with body fluids, skin, and cells. Moreover, they should keep their functionality, effectiveness, and safety. Additional material requirements for medical plastics devices could be found for the following product categories:[1]

1. Material characterization
2. Sterilization resistance
3. Chemical as well as lipid resistance
4. Extractables as well as leachable characterization
5. Hemocompatibility and biocompatibility
6. Stability and shelf life

Numerous devices must be packaged and sterilized either before distribution or usage.

## Sterilization with No Loss of Efficiency

All such medical health products with plastic as a base material should be sterilized with no loss of efficiency. Types of such products are surgical gloves and exam, suitable space garments, sample cups, wound care solutions, sutures, needles, syringes, catheters, drain bags, IV bags, substance delivery methods, surgery supplies, dental instruments, surgical instruments, implants, dialysis equipment, and mixture products.

## Materials Guide Highlights Thermoplastic's Medical Applications with Kydex

Supplier Curbell Plastics has posted a guide detailing the Kydex line's health uses of its thermoplastics. Inherently antimicrobial and chemically resistant, the content is usually utilized for medical unit housings and healthcare furniture. Kydex thermoplastic's manual, to disinfect health-related equipment in the hospitals, frequently uses reliable cleaning agents, particularly since the COVID-19 outbreak. As an outcome, the material is cracking and breaking at an accelerated speed.

Kydex thermoplastics enjoys a distinctive blend of polymers that provide medical equipment and device manufacturers the desired bodily durability against discoloration or brittleness from continuous chemical contact and wipe-down schedules, based on Curbell. Nearly all plastics utilize additive plasticizers, which provide a nutrient tool for microbial growth, stated Curbell. Nevertheless, Kydex thermoplastics don't include plasticizers in their chemical makeup, and the material prohibits fungal and bacterial growth.

Curbell supplies the material suitable for medical device manufacturers and hospital equipment providers with an outstanding thermoforming capability to create comprehensive part geometries. Injection-molded is usually effective at becoming thermoformed with Kydex thermoplastics. Curbell stated that Kydex sheet styles to deep draw produce far more consistent merchandise than some other thermoplastics, sometimes causing less rejected components.

# Key Factor of Success #3: The Critical Role of Technical Specifications

Several factors play a critical role in technical specifications.

## *Developing Assembled Medical Units*

The modern medical device-making companies are performing exclusively to promote the products. In developing a medical unit wherein assembly is needed, one needs to consider the component layout and the assembly process, the standard style, and procedure management. Factors such as part size, material, geometry, and end-user specifications are essential. The most important is to ensure the same results in the lab and a natural manufacturing environment. Several issues that may occur throughout the development process together need to rectify them with potential.

## Advanced Role in Technical Specifications

Several technical advances about generating innovative plastics for healthcare programs govern the healthcare plastic industry. The primary significant considerations found for healthcare plastics manufacturers are mainly: selecting the correct alternative, process strategies, and process management, general as well as joint component layout.

Developing a medical unit wherein assembly is required, one shall consider the component layout, the assembly process, the typical style, and the amount of procedure management. It also includes a few essential things- size, base material and specifications, geometrical components, and end-user stipulations. The material must behave the same in the laboratory and at the workshop.

Every day is increasing reliance on transparent plastic pharmaceuticals and medical products has produced remarkable breakthroughs. It improves the delivery of medical attention, and it allowed it to be more comfortable for a considerable number of individuals to live better and longer lives.

## Technical Specifications and the Integration of the Supply Chain

Considerable technical integration through different phases of the value chain is a demand of the marketplace. Selecting the correct alternative and process strategies, general and joint component layout, and process management have facilitated an integration throughout the value chain. HELM AG is an example of incorporating all four phases in the value chain out of raw material production to the manufacturing and plastic production of end-use items used by the hospitals and healthcare institutions such as private clinics.

This company organizes global supply chains with innovative and efficient logistics solutions and offers them to third parties. Using sophisticated warehousing solutions, associated value-added services, and intelligent networking of all transportation media, HELM guarantees consistent product transport to its professional partners' locations and sure deliveries to customers according to schedule.

# Key Factor of Success # 4: Key Role of Medical Grade Plastics

The quality of medical-grade plastic has recently become more an essential factor of success.

The concept of "medical grade" implies that the merchandise, anything they could be, is derived from a seller that runs under a physician's license. In a health plastic manufacturer situation, what this means is a medical director who oversees and regulates the used materials to fabricate the apparatus. Medical-grade polypropylene and medical-grade polycarbonate are two typical polymers used in several applications, from MRI casings to medical equipment.

## *Medical-Grade Plastics Benefits*

Medical-grade polymers are a crucial part of the worldwide healthcare ecosystem. Polymers come in a variety of surgical instruments, including catheters and implants. With a transparent comprehension of medical-grade plastics in mind, we need to check out a couple of benefits to provide the healthcare sector.

## Versatility

Healthcare plastic has a proper scope of healthcare uses, out of the transparent to the unexpected. Disposable health goods as bedpans, inhalation masks, and IV tubes have shifted from various other substances to transparent plastic in recent years. Today, plastic is utilized in several kinds and pill casings of inner implants, from catheters to joint substitutes. The majority of everything you see in a modern clinic room features plastic material.

## Easy Sterilization

Medical gear like medical tools is perfect for one-time use when made of healthcare plastic. The spread of unsafe diseases and infections was prevented by just getting rid of single-use tools after a process is finished. Nevertheless, additionally, there are different plastics used in medical devices with antimicrobial surfaces. These covers are best at both killing and repelling hazardous bacteria, even not frequently sterilized.

## Greater Safety

Since healthcare plastic is non-permeable and shatter-proof, it's a helpful alternative for safely transporting biohazardous substances—the safe removal of medical waste aids in preventing the spread of dangerous pathogens. Likewise, healthcare plastic is employed in tamper-proof caps, ensuring no foul play occurs in a patient's pharmaceuticals.

## Improved Quality of Life

Medical-grade plastics have helped to create the lives of amputees much comfortable. Since plastic can be highly personalized because of injection molding, an individual receives a little, durable prosthetic. Lots of plastics are hypoallergenic. Therefore, individuals with allergies to conventional health substances as latex are at a reduced risk of response during therapy.

## Cost-Effective

The number of uses, lower manufacturing costs, and medical plastics' longevity make it an advanced material sought after contemporary medicine investment. Metallic and glass products are susceptible to oxidation and shattering. Plastic is reluctant to both. Simultaneously, many plastic tools are created for single-use disposal, additional equipment designed to deal with repeated sterilizations, and last a good deal longer.

## Environmental and Eco-Friendly

Plastics are recyclable, which makes them the most eco-sustainable choice for medical equipment. It's significantly more comfortable for healthcare providers to meet up with their demanding medical-related uses and stay environmentally conscientious because of medical-grade plastics.

## Potential of Future Innovations

The healthcare plastic innovations presently being researched could provide more significant benefits to the healthcare industry. 3-D printing makes it easier to create inexpensive, comfortable and prosthetics. Researchers are currently testing an injectable plastic that might help carefully staunch bleeding because of internal trauma. The possibilities are numerous.

## Thermoplastic Medical Applications

### A Guide Detailing the Health Uses of the Kydex Line of Thermoplastics[2]

Kydex thermoplastics enjoy a distinctive blend of polymers that provide medical equipment and device manufacturers the desired bodily durability against discoloration or brittleness from continuous chemical contact and wipe-down schedules, based on Curbell.

Nearly all plastics utilize additive plasticizers, which provide a nutrient tool for microbial growth, stated Curbell. Nevertheless, Kydex thermoplastics don't include plasticizers in their chemical makeup, and the material is shown to prohibit fungal and bacterial growth.

Injection-molded is usually active at becoming thermoformed with Kydex thermoplastics. Kydex sheet styles to deep draw produce far more consistent merchandise than some other thermoplastics, sometimes causing less rejected components, stated Curbell.

# Key Factor of Success # 5: Continuous Product Development

## R&D to Create Advanced Products

The companies' recourse to new merchandise developments is one of the major strategies to achieve market growth. Also, key market players invest significantly in R&D to develop advanced products

A high level of competition is apt to strengthen customer purchasing power. Product quality, and cost competitiveness, are the main factors impacting the customer power decision. Increased production volumes and the simplicity of accessibility of healthcare plastics are anticipated to operate the customer energy within the next couple of years. Therefore, new product development is critical.

The suppliers resort to product developments that are new as one of the main strategies to achieve industry growth. Additionally, key industry players invest considerably in R&D to create advanced products.

## *Production Techniques to Introduce New Plastics*

These brand-new plastics are going to demand applicability. It means is that your design is going to be competitive and effectively thought out! The long term brings us an assortment of sensible plastics, self-healing plastics, and nanotechnology for individuals, profit, and the planet. But there's one thing we all know for sure; we've to change our designing methods and what this means is to change the development in raw materials, search for other online resources, alternatives, and production techniques.

## *The Case of SCG Chemicals*

### *Developing Medical Plastics*

One of the inventions that SCG Chemicals has been pushing much energy into developing is medical plastics. This step is valuable to society as it helps improve the standard of living and health of the people. Patients can get more comfortable and better access to medical treatments as plastic equipment is inexpensive and more comfortable for transportation to other places and does not break easily. Therefore, it is very suitable to deliver such material as blood bags, I.V. bags, and needles to town areas and the big cities' suburban.

Moreover, modernizations also make it more appropriate for patients and handlers to use the medical kit to ease their families. For example, peritoneal dialysis bags can also be used at home, so patients do not want to travel to the hospital. Apart from helping better people's lives, plastic medical innovations also help our country's economy reduce the number of imported thermoplastics and equipment from abroad. Mr. Yutan Jamaican, Managing Director of SCG Performance Chemicals Co. Ltd. (a subsidiary of SCG Chemicals) said that the government of a country like Thailand is looking forward to making the nation a medical hub with skilled doctors, advanced hospitals, reliable services, and kind heart nurses. To be exact, Thailand has all this but lacks medication and the proper medical equipment. SCG Chemicals moved forward in helping by developing medical equipment of good value and good quality production to be accessible to more patients and improve the population in the long run.

## Replacing Traditional Medical Equipment

People wonder whether plastics used in medical equipment are different from the everyday use of plastics. Most of them are yet not convinced the plastic is replacing the present material used in medical equipment. The general public is worried about the safety of plastic and health-hazard. Mr. Yutan kindly added more information regarding this issue. There are differences between regular plastics and plastics used in medical equipment.

The product matters a lot because plastic is intensively used in medical equipment. Every medical instrument goes through the process of sterilization. Every medical equipment design is essential. Medical treatment concerns patients' lives, and it needs to go through boiling with high centigrade

temperature and sterilization by use of chemicals like ethylene oxide and some through gamma rays. SCG Chemicals
plastics always go through the top existing sterilization
methods.

SCG needs a more advanced technology if talks in the
term of modern technology. The company SCG has done
tons of research and development in advancing medical
equipment. We need to regulate the excellence of production
in every single stage. It has to pass the standards of GMP
(good manufacturing practices) such as ISO-13485. GMP
conducts thorough quality control in every progression to
make sure nothing is polluted. SCG Chemicals is the foremost and the first plastics manufacturer in Asia that employs
ISO-13485 as we consider safety the most critical factor in
our production.

## A Move Forward with Innovative Service

Plastic innovations for medical treatments, as well as innovative services, is an identity of SCG Chemicals. SCG Chemicals
set up a design Catalyst to choose and design quality plastics
at every step of innovation. Catalyst is an innovative service
that makes us diverse from other chemical manufacturers. We
are the original manufacturer in ASEAN that provides this type
of service.

Our Carpal Tunnel Retractor (CTR) is a great example.
It has designed 'Design Catalyst' to answer all the other
innovator and suppliers of medical equipment's demands
and queries. We could substitute the material used for
operation from stainless steel to plastic and made innovation successful. This kit helps with the cutting process and
production costs. The best part is that it also lessens the
wound's size and surgical operation time from one hour to
eight minutes.

Today, reputed hospitals across the country have been using these kits in their operating rooms and are launched. These launches are considered the first medical innovation that has gained recognition worldwide. It has also received a prominent award from Switzerland.

## Notes

1. https://doi.org/10.1016/B978-0-8155-2027-6.10004-2.
2. www.plasticstoday.com/medical/new-materials-guide-high-lights-thermoplastic-s-medical-applications/53353726162890.

*Chapter 9*

# Strategic Perspective from Market Leaders

## HMC Polymers' Medical Applications

HMC Polymers' product Purell is the benchmark polypropylene used by global manufacturers for medical and pharmaceutical applications, including IV bottles, syringes, and pharmaceutical packaging. Regulatory requirements affect the manufacture of medical and pharmaceutical products making demands on medical devices and packaging. Purell is produced under near-pharmaceutical conditions and utilizes dedicated cleaning procedures for product logistics.

For the use of plastics in medical applications, the European Union has developed the European Pharmacopeia directive (EP-3.1.6) describing the use of "Polypropylene for Containers and Closures for Preparations for Parenteral and Ophthalmic Use." This directive provides guidelines and information to allow medical and pharmaceutical product manufacturers to make informed choices of the selection and use of plastics for medical and pharmaceutical applications.

DOI: 10.4324/9781003212898-9

# Baxter

The use of polymers biomaterials is increasing day by day. The biomaterials implanted in the body of living provide special prosthetic functions are for diagnostic, surgical, and therapeutic applications.

Baxter's strengths in the competition include its broad technological competence and its commitment to continuous scientific innovations. The combined know-how in the three core fields of medical products, pharmacy, and biotechnology sets Baxter apart from other medical and healthcare industries.

Technologies and scientific research disciplines are growing ever closer together. This research results in a growing number of new therapies that doctors can use to benefit their patients. Combining medical knowledge with modern technologies offers promising approaches to successfully tackle critical tasks such as avoiding medication errors and infections in hospitals. This can also improve the quality of life and clinical results in chronically ill people's care. Finally, this development also promotes the transfer of therapies from the hospital directly into the patient's living space.

Baxter operates research and development (R&D) centers worldwide, including Austria, Belgium, Japan, and the United States. Our future strategy in the area of R&D includes recombinant and plasma-based therapeutics as well as vaccines, measures of regenerative medicine, dialysis, and small-molecule pharmaceutical forms. The focus is also on optimized packaging systems, pioneering formulation techniques for pharmaceuticals, and new pharmaceutical blending processes.

## *Medical Plastics Technology*

When Baxter launched the first flexible plastic blood collection container on the market several decades ago, it changed how blood was taken. This also paved the way for the first elastic and plastic solution container for intravenous (IV) therapy. This product quickly became the widely accepted industry standard and is still the leader today. The MINI-BAG container systems for IV drugs and the flexible plastic containers for peritoneal dialysis (P.D.) followed later. It made mobile dialysis therapy possible for the first time. Today medical plastics are an integral part of numerous Baxter product lines. We successfully combined our medical plastics expertise with our biologics knowledge and presented a unique product in the market.

## Trinseo Medical Plastics

Trinseo is recognized for its leadership in chemical-resistant materials to combat Hospital Acquired Infections (HAI). We offer a platform of wear-resistant, high lubricated polycarbonate, ISO 10993 certified biocompatible glass-filled resins, and skin contact grades for applications with limited or non-invasive patient contact.

By supporting today's OEMs as they manufacture medical devices for required human interaction, Trinseo provides medical-grade resins for single-and multiple-use devices such as surgical instruments and IV drip chambers, drug delivery systems, diagnostic equipment housings, and medical wearables. The company is a technology leader and innovator. Our involvement with medical devices ranges from syringe barrels and lure locks to some of the most advanced applications supporting the evolution in 5-G Network technology that relies on cross-industry expertise.

Trinseo medical-grade products are manufactured with heightened attention to quality and consistency. Our global manufacturing and compounding facilities assure supply and operate according to cGMP or ISO 13485 standards. We also offer cleanroom manufactured polycarbonate to assure minimal particulate matter entering application workstreams.

Trinseo has a network of regional medical product stewards that supports customers with regulatory compliance to lower risk, increasing speed to market, and providing products so that innovators can continue to focus on improving healthcare delivery. Select from our resources to learn more about our products and their applications in the medical device marketplace, or contact us directly and let's discuss how we can work together.

## GW Plastics

Engineering, at its core, is about solving problems. GW Plastics has earned a reputation for developing highly reliable, innovative solutions at healthcare customers' complex. It can provide sophisticated needs—quickly, economically, and effectively. With global capabilities and over 60 years of industry expertise, GW Plastics wishes to become the logical single-source healthcare partner for a healthy life.

The core competencies of GW Plastics include thermoplastic molding and liquid silicone rubber/liquid injection molding (LSR/LIM), along with their dynamic capabilities in medical product development, Design for Excellence (DfX), Design for Manufacturing (DFM), and advanced contract manufacturing. They make GW Plastics the partner of choice for the world's most successful healthcare companies. Whether it's helping to develop a new healthcare product from the ground up, improving an existing product or process, or assisting with the medical regulatory process, the regular customers trust GW to deliver the right solution every time.

Medical device contract manufacturing and leading medical and healthcare companies around the globe turn to GW Plastics to extend their production capabilities. In addition to product development, precision molding, and in-house tooling expertise, the company offers complete turnkey contract assembly with a lean Six Sigma manufacturing approach.

# Saint-Gobain Medical Components

A world leader with unparalleled material expertise in silicone, thermoplastic elastomers, and fluoropolymers, Saint-Gobain is the processing expert in molding, extrusion, and all-encompassing custom fabrication for medical OEMs. The company is committed and leading the way through its global resources and technological expertise; it provides outstanding quality and exceptional value by developing innovative, high-performance solutions for medical devices. Backed by a rich history of advanced materials expertise, Saint-Gobain brings an unparalleled knowledge of high-performance polymers to the pharmaceutical market.

Saint-Gobain introduced several innovative practices such as the followings:

- Silicone for medical: Silicone is an ideal material for a variety of medical device applications. Engineers on the floor develop precise, consistently manufactured silicone parts through adopted custom compounding capability.
- Thermoplastics: Advanced processing ability allows a company to produce thermoplastic materials in a broad range of chemistries.
- Fluoropolymers: Saint-Gobain applies the extensive materials expertise of GW Plastics to maximize the properties of fluoropolymers and engineered materials.
- Other materials: GW Plastics develops unique material compounds and processing techniques to create custom formulations for specific user needs.

# Bibliography

Brodd, R. J. (n.d.). Comments on the History of Lithium-Ion Batteries. Retrieved from The Electrochemical Society website: www.electrochem.org/dl/ma/201/pdfs/0259.pdf

Cummings, P. T., & Glotzer, S. C. (2010). Inventing a New America through Discovery and Innovation in Science, Engineering, and Medicine. Retrieved from the World Technology Evaluation Center and the National Science Foundation website: www. wtec.org/sbes-vision/RDW-color-FINAL-04.22.10.pdf2010

Division of Injury Response at the National Center for Injury Prevention and Control (U.S.). (2006, January). Traumatic Brain Injury in the United States: Emergency Department Visits, Hospitalizations, and Deaths. Retrieved from Centers for Disease Control and Prevention, U.S. Department of Health and Human Services website: www.cdc.gov/ncipc/pub-res/tbi_in_us_04/tbipercent20inpercent20thepercent20us_jan_2006.pdf

Farrands, C. (1990). New Materials in Manufacturing Industry the Economist Intelligence Unit, Special Report 2026.

Finkelstein, E. A., Corson, P. S., & Miller, T. R. (2006). *The Incidence and Economic Burden of Injuries in the United States.* New York: Oxford University Press.

Froes, F. H. (1997). Is the Use of Advanced Materials in Sports Equipment Unethical? *JOM*, 15–19.

The Inter-Agency Composites Group. (2009). Technology Needs to Support Advanced Composites in the U.K. Retrieved from: http://avaloncsl.files.wordpress.com/2013/01/composites-tech-needs-nov-2009.pdf

International Competitiveness in the Advanced Materials Sector: The Case of Carbon Fibre. Retrieved from: www.academia.

  edu/1243204/International_Competitiveness_in_the_Advanced_
  Materials_Sectr_the_case_of_carbon_fibre

Jerome, S. B. (1998). Composite Material Advances in the Golf
  Industry. Retrieved from: www.iccm-central.org/Proceedings/
  ICCM12proceedings/site/papers/pap338.pdf

Lucintel. (2011). Creating the Equation for Growth. *SPEA ACCE
  (2011): Growth Opportunities in the Global Composites
  Industry*. Retrieved from: www.speautomotive.com/SPEA_CD/
  SPEA2011/pdf/KEY/K4.pdf

Markowitz, S. (2009). *The Advanced Materials Revolution:
  Technology and Economic Change in the Age of Globalization*.
  New York: John Wiley and Sons, Inc.

National Research Council (U.S.). (2008). *Integrated Computational
  Materials Engineering*. Washington, DC: The National
  Academies Press.

Network for Computation Nanotechnology. (2009). Nano HUB.
  Retrieved from National Science Foundation website: http://
  nanohub.org/

New Materials International. (2010). Trends in Advanced
  Composite Usage Observed during the Review of 2010 JEC
  Awards Applications. Retrieved from: www.newmaterials.
  com/News_Detail_Trends_in_advanced_composite_usage_
  observed_during_the_review_of_2010_jec_awards_
  applications_percent20_12463.asp#ixzz2tIcFS9Sz

OECD. (1990). *Advanced Materials: Policies and Technological
  Change*. Paris: OECD.

Porter, M. (1990). *The Competitive Advantage of Nations*. Springfield,
  MA: Macmillan.

President's Council of Advisors on Science and Technology. (2010,
  December). Realizing the Full Potential of Health Information
  Technology to Improve Healthcare for Americans: The Path
  Forward. Retrieved from Executive Office of the President web-
  site: www.whitehouse.gov/sites/default/files/microsites/ostp/
  pcast-health-it-report.pdf

PR Newswire. (2013). Growth Opportunities in Global Composites
  Industry 2011–2016. Retrieved from: www.prnewswire.com/
  news-releases/growth-opportunities-in-global-composites-
  industry-2011-2016-131970408.html

Rao, S., Imam, R., Ramanathan, K., & Pushpavanam, S. (2009).
  Sensitivity Analysis and Kinetic Parameter Estimation in a

Three-Way Catalytic Converter. *Industrial and Engineering Chemistry Research*, 8(48), 3779–3790. DOI:10.1021/ ie801244w

Russell, C. (1996). International Competitiveness in the Advanced Materials Sector: The Case of Carbon Fiber. A thesis was submitted to the University of Manchester for the degree of PhD in the Faculty of Science. Manchester: Policy Research in Engineering, Science & Technology.

Stuhmiller, J. H. (2008). *Blast Injury: Translating Research into Operational Medicine* (W. R. Santee, K. E. Friedl, & Walter Reed Army Medical Center Borden Institute, Eds.). TMM Publications.

Watt, E. O., & Outhred, H. R. (2006). *Strategies for the Adoption of Renewable Energy Technologies*. Oxford, UK: Eolss Publishers. Retrieved from: www.eolss.net/ebooks/ Samplepercent20Chapters/C08/E3-21-03-06.pdf

Whittingham, M. S. (1976, June). Electrical Energy Storage and Intercalation Chemistry. *Science, 192*(4244), 1126–1127. DOI:10.1126/science.192.4244.1126

World Technology Evaluation Center. (2009). WTEC Panel Report on International Assessment of Research and Development in Simulation-Based Engineering and Science. Retrieved from: www.wtec.org/sbes/SBES-GlobalFinalReport.pdf

# Index

Page numbers in *italics* indicate a figure and page numbers in **bold** indicate a table on the corresponding page.

Printed in the United States
by Baker & Taylor Publisher Services